From South Carolina: "Thank you, David, for writing such a powerful book, a book that has shown me what God has been trying to tell me for over thirty years!"

From Illinois: "Your book was challenging and excellent...Looking forward to your next book."

From Australia: "I feel awakened!...The truth I found in your book is not what we are hearing preached. It's like you have opened a door for me...I hope one day to see you speak in Australia."

From California: "The peace I felt when I was saved has not seemed to be what 'the church' is about...The hamster wheel of *doing* conflicts with the rest and peace being in the Lord offers...Thanks for putting out something that speaks to what I see in the Bible but as a newbie did not have the confidence to explore on my own."

From Michigan: "I read your book through for the second time. I'm so excited that God brought this before me...Thank you, God...My group will be ministering at a Michigan prison...I have so much more to bring to this ministry now...Awesome, isn't it?"

From New England: "Thank you for speaking out boldly. The truths you have selected do have the power to give Christians all they have been promised and all they've been looking for."

You Mean That Isn't in the Bible?

DAVID A. RICH

HARVEST HOUSE PUBLISHERS

EUGENE, OREGON

Cover by Dugan Design Group, Bloomington, Minnesota

Cover photo © Zbigniew Koscielniak

YOU MEAN THAT ISN'T IN THE BIBLE?
Copyright © 2008 by David A. Rich
Published by Harvest House Publishers
Eugene, Oregon 97402
www.harvesthousepublishers.com

Library of Congress Cataloging-in-Publication Data
Rich, David (David A.)
You mean that isn't in the Bible? / David A. Rich.
   p. cm.
ISBN-13: 978-0-7369-2138-1
ISBN-10: 0-7369-2138-9
1. Bible—Miscellanea. 2. Christianity—Miscellanea. 3. Common fallacies I. Title.
BS538.R47 2008
230.'041—dc22

2007034820

Printed in the United States of America

08 09 10 11 12 13 14 15 16 / VP-SK / 12 11 10 9 8 7 6 5 4 3 2 1

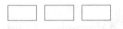

To my wife, Brenda, who has stood by me (albeit sometimes rolling her eyes) as I've challenged people as to what they believe and why they believe it. Words cannot express my thankfulness for having you in my life.

Acknowledgments

I'd like to thank the entire team at Harvest House for all you've done for this book and *7 Biblical Truths You Won't Hear in Church*. You are truly among the best groups of people I've ever worked with.

CONTENTS

The Truth Is Making a Comeback   9

1. How Religion Has Gotten Off Track   13

Ten Popular Beliefs You Won't Find in God's Book

2. Belief #1: There Are Many Roads to Heaven   27

3. Belief #2: When We Die, We Become Angels   37

4. Belief #3: God Helps Those Who Help Themselves . .   47

5. Belief #4: God Wants You to Be Rich   57

6. Belief #5: Christian Aren't Perfect, Just Forgiven   67

7. Belief #6: We Are God's Co-Pilots   77

8. Belief #7: Pray Hard and God Will Answer   87

9. Belief #8: God and Satan Are Battling It Out   97

10. Belief #9: God Is Not a Micromanager 107

11. Belief #10: Everyone Has Their Own Free Will 115

Why God's Truth Is Better

12. Another Reformation 127

Beyond the Beliefs 133

More Beliefs to Explore and Examine 137

Notes 147

JT • GOD IS NOT A MICROMANAGER • EVERYONE HAS THEIR OWN FREE WILL • THERE AR
Y ROADS TO HEAVEN • WHEN WE DIE WE BECOME ANGELS • GOD HELPS THOSE WHO HEL
SELVES • GOD WANTS YOU TO BE RICH • CHRISTIANS AREN'T PERFECT, JUST FORGIVEN
RE GOD'S CO-PILOTS • PRAY HARD AND GOD WILL ANSWER • GOD AND SATAN ARE BATTLIN
JT • GOD IS NOT A MICROMANAGER • EVERYONE HAS THEIR OWN FREE WILL • THERE AR
Y ROADS TO HEAVEN • WHEN WE DIE WE BECOME ANGELS • GOD HELPS THOSE WHO HEL
SELVES • GOD WANTS YOU TO BE RICH • CHRISTIANS AREN'T PERFECT, JUST FORGIVEN
RE GOD'S CO-PILOTS • PRAY HARD AND GOD WILL ANSWER • GOD AND SATAN ARE BATTLIN

The Truth Is
Making a Comeback

I am humbled and honored you've picked up this book and have begun reading it. As with my first book, *7 Biblical Truths You Won't Hear in Church,* you were probably struck by the title and became a little curious as to what might be inside.

This is the sister book to *7 Truths.* Whereas that book addressed truths that are often "missing in action" in today's churches, this book addresses popular beliefs people have come to believe are actually in the Bible. Don't be surprised if you find yourself saying, "You mean that isn't in the Bible?" as you read forward. Many of these popular beliefs are so rooted in our culture that it's hard to determine how they got started, but somehow, some way, and somewhere along the way, popularity has become more important than truth. Individuality has become more important than integrity, and doing and believing in what feels right has become more important than doing and believing in what *is* right.

I am not too proud to admit that part of my aim is to shock you into reading. In this case, the end justifies the means. In fact, I've often called my small ministry a "shock ministry," inasmuch as I like to challenge people to find the truth. We have arrived at a place in history where, in an effort to respect whatever anyone might believe, we have blurred the lines between absolute truth and whatever sounds and feels right in someone's personal belief system.

Will You Like What You Find?

The popular beliefs I examine in the book you hold are popular for a varying number of reasons. Some are popular simply because of longevity. Some other popular beliefs became popular because a prominent American said so, and others just because they seem logical. Finally, there are a few that are popular simply because we want them to be true. Whatever the reason, being popular doesn't make them biblically correct. We've believed them so long we've come to believe they're actually in the Bible.

It's crucial at this time in our religious history that we get back to our biblical roots. It's crucial that we stand up for absolute truth. I believe we may be headed for another reformation—and it's about time we know what we believe, and as importantly, why we believe what we believe. I will warn you up front that if you're looking for a warm and fuzzy book you can read without much thought, this is not it. In fact, you may even get downright riled up at some of the things I have to say.

That's okay. I don't expect everyone to agree with everything I write about. Changing beliefs is the mental equivalent to climbing Mt. Everest. What I do expect is to stimulate you enough to provoke you to more study so as to become crystal clear as to the things you believe. I want you to be driven to the Word. The Bible has been and remains the ultimate source for wisdom and truth.

I am not, nor do I even remotely consider myself, a theologian. I am simply a believer who is compelled to share some of the life-changing truths I've been blessed to discover over the last decade or so. I'll never forget the night my journey began.

I was sitting in a restaurant in San Francisco over ten years ago having dinner with a few of my professional speaker colleagues. Somehow the conversation got on religion. Glenna Salsbury, to whom I've dedicated *7 Truths,* seemingly came out of the blue and hit me right between the eyes with a few truths I had never heard before. The things she said I just knew couldn't be true. They didn't feel right, and after all, I grew up in the Christian church. I had considered myself a believer for as long as I could remember. I couldn't recall ever hearing some of the things she was claiming were in the Bible. I spent that night scouring my hotel Gideon Bible to try to find scriptural evidence to prove her wrong. I didn't get much sleep. You see, the more I looked, the more the Bible seemed to prove she was right. Glenna drove me to the Scriptures, and I fell in love with what I've found.

Since that night, I've come to *know* my friend was right. How could I have missed these truths and why doesn't everyone see them? I still ask myself those questions all the time. Glenna was my catalyst just as I hope this book can be yours. It turns out that as much as I admire and appreciate Glenna, she is not a rare biblical genius. She is just one in a long line of believers who has discovered these truths and felt compelled to pass them on. The most heartwarming compliments I can receive are when I hear from a reader that they too have been hit between the eyes, discovered peace like never before, and can't wait to share the good news.

I invite you to replace those tired old popular beliefs with real, life-changing biblical truths.

Don't be surprised if that happens to you. But also don't be surprised if it doesn't. I just put it out there and let the chips fall where they may. I'm just following God's leading. What He does is entirely up to Him. As you will find out, I like to call myself a "sovereignist." I know that word hasn't existed before, but it most accurately describes my theology. I believe God is the one and only. He is in charge of every little thing that happens. Nothing happens outside of His providence. He likes being God, and the only way to find true peace in this world is to lean entirely and completely on Him.

So what He does with this book and where He takes you is His domain. I can only thank you and urge you to spread the word. I invite you to replace those tired old popular beliefs with real, life-changing biblical truths, ones that can really make a difference. There is such a thing as absolute truth and I believe it's about to make a comeback!

JT • GOD IS NOT A MICROMANAGER • EVERYONE HAS THEIR OWN FREE WILL • THERE AR
Y ROADS TO HEAVEN • WHEN WE DIE WE BECOME ANGELS • GOD HELPS THOSE WHO HEL
SELVES • GOD WANTS YOU TO BE RICH • CHRISTIANS AREN'T PERFECT, JUST FORGIVEN
RE GOD'S CO-PILOTS • PRAY HARD AND GOD WILL ANSWER • GOD AND SATAN ARE BATTLIN
JT • GOD IS NOT A MICROMANAGER • EVERYONE HAS THEIR OWN FREE WILL • THERE AR
Y ROADS TO HEAVEN • WHEN WE DIE WE BECOME ANGELS • GOD HELPS THOSE WHO HEL
SELVES • GOD WANTS YOU TO BE RICH • CHRISTIANS AREN'T PERFECT, JUST FORGIVEN
RE GOD'S CO-PILOTS • PRAY HARD AND GOD WILL ANSWER • GOD AND SATAN ARE BATTLIN

CHAPTER 1

How Religion Has Gotten Off Track

There's a church in my hometown that is growing by leaps and bounds. It is by far the biggest church in the area, and bear in mind, I live in the heart of the Bible Belt where church attendance is among the highest in the country. It is like a growing number of churches called megachurches. There are a reported 1200-plus megachurches in the United States alone. In 1990, there were only 350.

I am certain that there is a church like this one where you live. They serve donuts and coffee in their pre-worship area that has all the amenities of a luxury hotel lobby. If you're running behind, and are not one of the early birds who have secured a seat in the worship center, there are "overflow" rooms equipped with huge video monitors and sound systems that would make many concert arenas envious. They offer valet parking, and the city has even assigned a police officer to conduct traffic to assist the thousands who attend one of their many services.

What's Going On in There?

Don't get me wrong. I don't have a problem with any of this. I have a problem with what goes on *inside* many of these churches. Religion has become big business. Church leaders are media superstars, and worshippers have become their customers. All too often, the message from the pulpit resembles something straight from corporate boardrooms and association conventions. I should know. I've spent 21 years speaking at such events. I've given thousands of presentations on how to improve one's lot in life. I have been squarely in the middle of the multibillion-dollar self-help movement that began decades ago with Earl Nightingale, Dale Carnegie, and Norman Vincent Peale. Along with the tens of thousands of others who call themselves speakers, trainers, and consultants, there are hundreds of presentations that take place every day. I, myself, have spoken for over one million people in my 20-plus years. It's an impressive number, but there are many other speakers who speak to a million people annually!

While I have focused on selling and customer service, there's a speech for almost every human situation, condition, and shortcoming. There's no shortage of expertise and diversity in the world of professional speaking. The one thing we all have in common, however, is the ability to motivate and inspire. Speakers try to inspire people to try harder, do better, and to find the strength from deep inside to hang on through tough, trying times. I've been known to use great movie lines and old clichés, like "You can do it"; "The customer is always right"; and "Success is a choice."

People like to hear positive messages and that's precisely how and why megachurches have grown so large. Religion has gotten into the self-help business, and they are simply responding to what their customer wants. The customer is always right and today's churchgoer wants to be empowered. Churches are in the business of "religious empowerment." Inspiring Christians to be better Christians is big business similar to inspiring salespeople to be better salespeople, or managers to be better at leading their troops. They want to feel good. Combine this with a church's desire to increase the membership ranks, and you've got the recipe for a megachurch.

Unfortunately biblical truth often takes a backseat in the attempt not to offend anyone, which is puzzling to me in light of the fact that the Bible is the most politically incorrect book of all time. Sermons that are easy to understand and digest will always attract more people than a sermon on one of the Bible's more complex issues. That's one of Dale Carnegie's lessons. Dale once wrote that honey attracts more bees than vinegar, and churches have adopted that philosophy whole-heartedly. A recent sermon that was advertised in our local paper was: "God wants you to be happy!" Who wouldn't want to hear that one? It appeals to the most basic of human desires, the pursuit of happiness. In fact, any one of the popular beliefs that I will discuss in this book could be (and probably was) the subject of a sermon at a church somewhere this past week!

So what's so bad about that? Well, nothing, if the teaching is balanced, properly credited, and rooted in actual Scripture. The problem is that it is often none of the above.

Where Is Balance Needed?

Let's look at the balanced issue first. Fox News has carved quite a niche for themselves by calling themselves "fair and balanced." One could argue the validity of that claim, but it's hard to argue their results. They often win the ratings war and more and more people are tuning in to see the counterpoint to opinions and biases that are commonplace on network news. In regard to Christian teaching, it is important to note that I am not speaking of cultural or worldly balance, or anything that might compromise scriptural truth. Worldly balance is not a good thing. For instance, more and more pastors are inviting leaders of radically different faiths to speak to their congregations. They argue balance. They argue it's a good thing to hear all sides of the religious spectrum, explore what's out there.

I disagree. Christianity is not a logical argument. It's a supernatural occurrence. It happens with the heart and goes to the brain, not the other way around. Listening to dissenting points of view may be interesting to some, but it's subjecting (and lowering) belief to an intellectual argument. I relate it to a married person going to a singles event to see what might be out there. They might argue that it's good to test your relationship and explore other options. Love, like faith, is a not a result of weighing the pros and cons. It's something from deep within, a heartfelt conviction. Why would I want to hear someone speak on why the Earth is flat if I believe with all my heart that it isn't? What would I gain except to feel sorry for the unenlightened presenter? No, that kind of worldly balance is not what I am referring to. I am referring to balance of biblical truth and teaching, and it all begins with the question of man's responsibility.

Theologians have debated for centuries the question of human agency. That is, what and how much is determined by man, and how much is determined by God. There is a balance. One can find as many passages from Scripture to support both sides. God commands us to do certain things, yet Scripture also tells us that God is not served by human hands. Which is true?

The answer of course is both. Man does play a role, but I believe not nearly as big a role as man think he does. I often use the analogy of a parent walking a child across a busy intersection. The parent has a grip on the child's hand and the child has a grip on the parent's hand. Two grips, two perspectives. The most critical question is, whose grip does the safety of the child depend on? While both grips are important, the safety and well-being of the child is determined by the parent's grip. If your children were anything like my children, they often didn't even grip back. I had to clutch their hands so tightly their fingertips turned white. I had to do that to fully protect them. I knew that had I loosened my grip, they might break free and get hit by a car.

The Bible teaches truths from both grip perspectives. There are countless passages that teach and even warn us how to have a better, tighter grip on the Father, and countless more on how we can feel completely safe and secure in the Father's grip. The problem is that churches tilt too heavily in the direction of the child's grip. Sermons that exhort us and warn us how to have a tighter grip and a better relationship with God dominate the religious landscape.

Lack of Balance = Lack of Motivation

It is important to note at this point that I am not antichurch. I go to a wonderful church and have spoken in many churches that are unquestionably doing far more good than bad. I just feel compelled to balance the scale. If more sermons on how to have a better grip on the Father would end with a peaceful reassurance that we cannot wiggle from His grip, I might not have a ministry.

But I do. I seek balance in Christian teaching. For every sermon on resisting the devil, there should be one on God's dominance over evil. For every sermon on man's responsibility of spreading the gospel, there should be one on God's ultimate design. For every sermon on repentance, there should be one on the final work of the cross. For every sermon on tithing, there should be one on using the gifts God gave you. For every sermon on things we should be doing, there should be one on resting in Christ. For every sermon on how the world is morally deteriorating, there should be one on trusting God.

You get the picture. I crave religious balance. The human side of me wants empowerment and help on gripping tighter, but without balance, it leaves people feeling empty and sometimes defeated. I can't tell you how many people I've met and interviewed through my travels that have become disillusioned with church going. They leave on a temporary high only to deflate come Monday morning. It's a phenomenon I am familiar with.

Moments after a motivational speech, audiences experience a rush of adrenaline. It can sometimes last days. It can cause a spike in sales, or the energy to complete a task, but motivational levels eventually return to pre-speech levels. It's normal. An audience member once confronted a famous colleague of mine, Zig Ziglar, on why motivational speeches were even necessary, given that they're only temporary. His reply was legendary. He said that baths were only temporary as well but we need one of those every day!

> I've met too many people who avoid church because it leaves them feeling guilty, ashamed, and depressed.

Motivation, even Christian motivation, is a good thing, but without balance it can also be harmful. Let me give you an example. If a speaker is trying to teach someone who is inherently shy and timid how to be an aggressive salesperson, it may be a waste of time. Although that person may pick up a trick or two or have momentary flashes of sales brilliance, it's not in the person's nature to be consistently outgoing. I often tell clients that I can't teach a cat to bark. No amount of training can get a cat to bark. No amount of training can get a person to be something they're not. Trying to make them something they're not will only leave them feeling defeated and inadequate.

The same is true with our spiritual life. I've met too many people who avoid church because it leaves them feeling guilty, ashamed, and depressed. I met a woman recently who claimed to be a believer but she couldn't understand how God could love her because she'd recently had an affair. I also met a man who lives in sheer poverty who told me that God was punishing him because he hadn't given much money to the church. A recent e-mail I received came from a teenager who wanted so badly to make God proud of him, but he had developed a weekend drinking habit. He wrote that it takes him until Wednesday to get over the guilt and begin talking to God again, only to repeat the cycle on Friday night.

These are examples of what can happen with an overabundance of child's grip teaching. The world is craving to know God's got them, that God is fully in charge, and that He is the only one who can change circumstances.

It comes down to giving credit where credit is due. Man takes too much credit and churches put too much stock in man's efforts.

As churches grow, their need to attract new members becomes more important. Deep doctrinal learning often takes a back seat to more general, don't-rock-the-boat, "spiritual-lite" entertainment. This may increase the ranks, but it leaves many believers feeling empty at the end of the service. A recent study conducted by LifeWay Research shows that more and more people are switching places of worship without a residential move. When asked why they left their old church, 58 percent said it was because their old church failed to engage their faith. It simply wasn't fulfilling their needs.

Crediting Your Source

Learning and being challenged has been replaced by messages aimed at the unchurched. As a result, more and more churches are performing altar calls at the end of the sermon. If you're not familiar with an altar call, you certainly have never been to a church in the South. An altar call is an invitation to come forward and proclaim Christ as your Savior. It can be a joyous time. I actually look forward to seeing new believers take that step. It's a big step. For many people, they'd rather get 20 stitches than have to stand before hundreds of people and profess something as personal as their faith. That's why I enjoy it so much. I know it takes a lot of courage.

But what exactly are we celebrating? Are we celebrating their courage? Are we celebrating their decision to join the church? Are we celebrating their proclamation that Jesus is Lord? Perhaps all of the above—and all that's wonderful, but what about giving the glory and credit to God? Pastors like to congratulate the new believer and invite everyone to come down after the service and welcome them into the club, but what about God? God sometimes isn't even mentioned.

"Congratulations, Johnny" should be replaced with "Thank you, Jesus!" Instead of high praises for the new believer and a passing comment about God, there should be high praises for God and a passing comment about the new believer. They should be patted on the back for their public display of courage and confession, but the strength for the courage and the changed heart came from God. He deserves the credit and, in my opinion, all the glory. Not some of the glory—*all* the glory. I don't want God to share the spotlight; I want God to have it all.

Now some of you might be saying, "Hold on, David. You might be getting all worked up over a minor technicality. Does it really matter in the long run?" My answer is a resounding *yes*. It matters! After I got finished speaking at a conference on grace a few years ago, a fellow speaker approached me with this same question. He said he preferred to "major in the majors, and minor in the minors."

In other words, let's keep our eyes on the *big* picture, and not split hairs over the minute details. Using my example of the altar call, he felt the big picture was that the world had a new believer and who gets the credit isn't as important as welcoming that new believer with open arms.

I guess that sounds okay, but to me, who gets the credit and glory isn't a small detail. To me, it's the other way around. The fact that the world welcomed a new believer is secondary to the work God performed in that person.

Let me put it another way: God's work is major. Human performance is minor. The world celebrates human performance. The worldly perspective is a human perspective. What we do for a living, where we live, what kind of car we drive, where we have been, what we've achieved, who we know, how many kids we have, what we believe, what things we like, and how we feel—these are the questions that define us. These are humanly relevant issues. These are child's-grip conversations.

What if we inserted God into the equation in the above questions? Instead of asking someone what they do for a living, ask them what God is having them do at this moment. Instead of asking someone where they've been, ask them where God has taken them. Instead of asking someone how many kids they have, ask them how many kids has God blessed them with. It may seem a bit unusual, but it's more accurate. It's the real majors. It's giving credit where credit is really due. It's taking the focus off man and placing it squarely where it belongs, with God. Let's not talk so much about what man is doing, but rather where God is leading us.

Help Yourself!

This may seem minor, but it's completely major. I get the impression that many churches would prefer to keep the focus on us, instead of on God. They want to talk about what we *should* be doing rather than trusting that God will take us where He wants us. I sometimes feel like churches condone guilt or shame if it causes us to be better

Christians. If guilt causes us to take a more active role in church func-
tions, then so be it. If shame causes us to throw a few more dollars in
the offering plate, that's okay. If peer pressure keeps us coming to worship service, that's what really matters. These beliefs are certainly not
openly admitted, but behind closed doors may be another thing.

Again, I am not indicting all churches and I am not antichurch,
but the statistics are worth noting.
According to statistics posted by
the Barna Group on their Web
site, 80 percent of all adults in the
U.S. call themselves Christians.

> You can get your fill of religious
> self-help...without ever owning,
> much less opening, a Bible.

Yet only 45 percent say they are "born again." Further, and even more
telling, only half of those who claimed to be "born again" said they
prayed to God, read from the Bible, and attended a worship service
in the past week.

What does this say? While there are several conclusions we can
draw from these statistics, it tells me that churches aren't necessarily
preaching to the choir. In other words, actual attendance doesn't translate into actual believers. Religion has gotten off track and churches
may be missing the mark. More and more people are going to church,
but the numbers may be misleading. Churches are trying to broaden
their reach and appeal, and in the effort to do so, biblical truth is
getting compromised. Fewer and fewer people believe in absolute
truth.

It is not unusual to attend megachurch worship and not even
hear one reference to a scriptural passage. Many of them talk about
Scripture in general terms but never refer to an actual passage. In a
completely unsubstantiated claim, I'll bet most attendees of a megachurch never even bring their Bibles to the service. I might go one
step further and broaden that to include all churchgoers in all kinds
of churches.

There may not be any statistics to back that up, but ask yourself
that question right now: Do you consistently bring your Bible to worship services, and if you do, do you open it? The upshot is that the Bible

is not necessary to attend church. You can get your fill of religious self-help, which may or may not be grounded in Scripture, without ever owning, much less opening, a Bible.

That's what this book is all about. This book talks about ten beliefs many think are biblically based. You may even come to believe them as a result of a church service somewhere in your past. The reaction I've gotten from people as I discuss these beliefs is, "You mean that isn't in the Bible?"

Tackling the Scary Stuff

For me, it's all about biblical truth. Whether that truth sounds right to me humanly or not is irrelevant. A well-respected pastor of a fairly large and outwardly successful church once confided in me that he purposely stays away from the more divisive truths of the Bible. According to his admission, the truths that go against human wisdom and may seem hard for us to understand are scary to talk about. It is his contention that tackling the tougher truths may hurt attendance and that his church had an emphasis on inclusion rather than being divisive.

I can't help but think of Jack Nicholson's famous line from the movie *A Few Good Men:* "You can't handle the truth." I think some churches think we can't handle the truth. After all, churches are a business and no business would do anything they thought would hurt sales. I don't believe this is an isolated philosophy. Many may not admit it, but it's good for church business to major in the majors and not worry about the minors. It's almost like a religious smorgasbord. Take what feels good to you and leave the other stuff alone. Take the parts of the Bible that sound right to our human perspective, and let's chalk up the harder-to-understand truths as the mysteries of God. If it doesn't sound right to us, then it simply must not be for us to understand—so why talk about it?

That's how inaccurate truth gets circulated. Someone, somewhere, says something that sounds right to us at the time and before we know it, we're repeating it to someone else. Most Christians know only what they've heard their pastor say. That is scary on many levels. Not that I believe pastors are saying wrong things, but rather they are being too careful on what they do say. If the goal is be popular and appeal to the masses, you can't say everything you want to say. The truth gets tempered, perhaps not deliberately, but by the very mission of the church to be inclusive.

My mission is a bit different. I feel led to carry the torch for the less popular biblical truths. I've always lived by the thought that if you try to stand for too much, you end up standing for nothing. I've been accused of being unbalanced myself. Some argue that I only teach truths from the Father's grip at the expense of human responsibility in the child's grip. That may be true, but not because I don't think our grip is important. Our grip is important, but if it wouldn't be for our Father's grip, we'd wiggle away and get hurt.

I choose to glory in the Father's grip. My grip doesn't give me peace. My grip is often rather questionable, but God's always got me, and He's got you too. Let's glory and find peace in that. As we begin this exploration into popular beliefs, remember this: Popular beliefs may sound good on the surface. If they didn't, they never would have become popular. But only absolute biblical truth is life-changing.

Ten Popular Beliefs
You Won't Find
in God's Book

| GOD IS NOT A MICROMANAGER • EVERYONE HAS THEIR OWN FREE WILL • THERE AR
ROADS TO HEAVEN • WHEN WE DIE WE BECOME ANGELS • GOD HELPS THOSE WHO HEL
SELVES • GOD WANTS YOU TO BE RICH • CHRISTIANS AREN'T PERFECT, JUST FORGIVEN •
RE GOD'S CO-PILOTS • PRAY HARD AND GOD WILL ANSWER • GOD AND SATAN ARE BATTLIN
T • GOD IS NOT A MICROMANAGER • EVERYONE HAS THEIR OWN FREE WILL • THERE AR
ROADS TO HEAVEN • WHEN WE D   NGELS • GOD HELPS THOSE WHO HEL
SELVES • GOD WANTS YOU TO BE RICH • CHRISTIANS AREN'T PERFECT, JUST FORGIVEN •
RE GOD'S CO-PILOTS • PRAY HARD AND GOD WILL ANSWER • GOD AND SATAN ARE BATTLIN

| CHAPTER 2 |

BELIEF #1

There Are Many Roads to Heaven

Perhaps the most damaging of the popular beliefs that simply isn't true is the one that there are many roads that lead to heaven. This is pure worldly, political correctness and is quite popular. Anyone who watches even a little television knows that it is popular and politically correct to believe that there are many ways to the afterlife. The belief is cloaked in such phrases like, "whatever you believe," and references to a "higher power." Many will use words like *fate* and *destiny* instead of the more politically incorrect words like *God* and *sovereignty*.

All of this comes from intellectualism. It comes from an inflated, "puffed up" image of man's worth. If we can't see it, touch it, experience it, and prove it, we have trouble believing it. Faith, and certainly Christian faith, is a completely different animal. It's the exact opposite. Popular beliefs also come from believing Christianity is like all other religions in the world. The truth is that it's not even a religion. Religion is a term that is man-made. I believe there is religion, and then there is Christ. Christ came to defy, unite, and obliterate religion. Contrary to popular belief, Christ is the only road to heaven.

I guess I could end the chapter with that, but as with all popular beliefs, it is important to do three things. First, talk about how and why it's become so popular; second, what beliefs feed into it; and lastly, counter it with solid biblical truth. *Biblical truth is always better than worldly wisdom.*

It Sounds Good to Me...

Let's begin with why it's popular to believe many roads lead to heaven. This belief, like many of the popular beliefs, stems from something I call *humanism,* or *intellectualism.* I will refer to these terms often. While there might be alternate definitions, I define humanism as the arrogance and vanity of man. If it makes sense to man, it must be right. We tend to interpret everything through the filter of humanism. I guess that makes sense because we are, after all, human. We can't interpret anything any other way. Dogs see the world through canine-colored glasses, and we as human beings see the world through our own self-defined filter. Boys see things as only boys can see them, girls see things as only girls can see them, fathers see things as only fathers can see things, mothers see things through a mother's eye, and so on. It's natural and it's the only thing we can do. The damage occurs when we try to interpret God through the eyes of man.

I say damaging because God does not play by our rules. He isn't subject to the laws of the land and His conclusions were not based on life experience. His ways are not our ways.[1] As humans we place a lot of importance on life experience, worldly wisdom, and the trappings of human success. We have an educational system that goes from grades 1 to 12, and then have a higher educational system after that. People get labeled based on where they fall in the numbering grid. The higher the number, the smarter you are presumed to be, and the more money and worth you command in the marketplace. Resumes are worldly scorecards, outlining the extent of our education and the job titles we've held. The longer we've been at places of employment, the better. The more important the titles we've had, the better.

Accumulated knowledge may affect how we're seen in the eyes of man, but it has nothing to do with how we're seen in God's eyes. The world keeps score with things accumulated. The bigger your house, the more important you must be. The longer and farther you travel for your vacation, the more important you must be. The more cars in your driveway, the more important you must be. The bigger the engagement diamond, the more you must love your future mate. These are all signs of worldly success and how we're seen in the eyes of man, but they have nothing to do with how we're seen in God's eyes. These are man's rules and man's value system, but it's not God's.

Money is a huge part of the human experience, but not to God. Money may be a sign of worldly success, but not to God. We'll cover money more extensively in a later chapter, but suffice it to say that worldly wealth does not translate to heavenly wealth. Big, wealthy churches are not necessarily right with God. Television evangelists, who ask for money to reach more people in the name of God, may not even know God.

Worldly wisdom and worldly success is humanism and should not be equated to how God sees things. God cannot be understood through our worldly system. In this world, a lot of importance is placed on fairness. Our court system is based on applying the same rules for everyone. It must be fair. It's a good system, but it's not how God operates. God is not the supreme judge making sure everyone plays by fair measures. It's how some may see God, but it's not accurate. God often doesn't seem fair by our standards. There's no due process with God. It's His way, period.

We often get caught up trying to define the way God operates by worldly standards. Something as big and important as how to get to heaven certainly must be fair. There must be due process and a logical system in place for people of all faiths. It must pass the smell test. You know the smell test—it must seem right to us. If it doesn't seem right, it must not be right. Society has applied the smell test to the question of going to heaven. It doesn't seem right that good, honest people don't go to heaven. It makes sense that if you lead a good life and are a good person, a loving God cannot and will not find you in contempt. This is the worldly, politically correct view of heaven.

The problem is, it's not biblical. It's popular, but it's not scriptural. Before we can go any further, we must come to this basic conclusion,

God does not operate under humanism. Riches in this life do not translate into heavenly riches. The system the world uses is not the system that God uses, and we cannot understand God by what sounds right to us. If it were possible for us to completely understand God and all He does, He would not be God.

The very idea of God is something we'll barely appreciate this side of heaven. God can only be understood through faith. It's not scientific, intellectual, or logical. "Many roads to heaven" sounds fair and sounds logical, but any Christian needs to reject this notion every time it comes up. This popular belief is an attack on our faith. It may be politically correct, but it's against the two biggest truths of the Christian faith. Those two truths are 1) the Bible is true and 2) Jesus is God. To believe that many roads lead to heaven one must believe both that the Bible is not accurate and Jesus was not God.

The Bible as a Roadblock

Let's look at the issue of biblical accuracy first. The argument against biblical accuracy centers on the fact that it was written by mortal man and thus must contain errors. There's even a growing number of people who believe the Bible is metaphoric and not to be taken literally. This is of course addressed by Scripture in 2 Timothy 3:16 that reads, "All Scripture is given by inspiration of God, and is profitable for doctrine, for reproof, for correction, for instruction in righteousness, that the man of God may be complete, thoroughly equipped for every good work." Basically that verse says that the Bible was not man's idea and handiwork, it was God's—and that God equipped them with the tools needed to get the job done.

You might be saying, sure, that's what the Bible says, but if you don't believe the Bible, you won't believe what it says. Well, I understand, but take the Bible out of the equation. Haven't there been times when you did something perfectly and wondered how you did it? Think of a time when you completed a task and afterward took amazing pride in your work. If we're honest, we can think of a few times that we did something that we could never repeat. We weren't sure how we did it and knew that all the pieces had to come together perfectly to make it happen, and they did. You may not have thought of God, but your work was perfect. Who hasn't made this comment at some point in their life, "I don't know how I did it!" We all have.

That's what happened with the Bible. The writers of the Bible may or may not have known where their inspiration was coming from, but they were led to write and they knew it was perfect. I can imagine Paul looking over his work and thinking, *Where did that come from?*

It reminds me of the story in Exodus 4 where God commanded Moses to lead the people of Israel out of Egypt. Moses, in verse 10, said, "O my LORD, I am not eloquent, neither before or since You have spoken to Your servant; but I am slow of speech and slow of tongue." Moses was saying words we've all said at one time: "I can't do that." But in the next verse, God said, "Who has made man's mouth? Or who makes the mute, the deaf, the seeing, or the blind? Have not I, the LORD? Now therefore, go and I will be with your mouth and teach you what to say." God was saying to Moses, *Yeah, you can't do it, but I can.* God worked through Moses. Moses was not a perfect man. He was mortal, but in this instance, he performed his duty perfectly and led his people out of Egypt. He had divine help.

The writers of the Bible were mortal men. They were not perfect, but in this instance, their writings were perfect. They had divine help. Unless you don't even believe in God, you must conclude that people can do anything if they have God's help. Therefore, it is more than possible that the Bible may be exactly as God wanted it to be.

The other argument against the Bible is that there are contradictory statements made, that it's all how one interprets what they read. Well, it is true that people will sometimes only see what they want to see, and that different interpretations may result. However, God's Word does not contradict itself. That doesn't mean that two passages held side by side may not appear to say opposite things. There are plenty of passages that appear to contradict each other, but a closer look at the context in which they were written and the full text of the entire Bible reveals God is incredibly consistent.

In fact, it's more of a miracle to believe that dozens of different men, at different times, at different places, in different circumstances, could write things that not only are amazingly consistent, but are very supportive of each other as well. Look at 2 Peter 1:20-21, which speaks directly to this argument: "No prophecy of Scripture is of any private interpretation, for prophecy never came by the will of man, but holy men of God spoke as they were moved by the Holy Spirit." This says that although man may indeed interpret the Bible differently, Scripture was not intended that way. God directed, man wrote. It's that simple.

> If God can create all the miraculous variety of nature and all its beauty, then He can surely preserve a single book.

Then there's the argument about time—that through the years, after translation after translation, the Bible's original meaning is compromised. I am flabbergasted at this one. If God can create life and the miraculous functioning of the human body, then God surely can preserve His writings through the years. If God can create the Earth, the universe, and the miraculous positioning of the sun to serve as our energy source, He can surely preserve a few words. If God can create all the miraculous variety of nature and all its beauty, then He can surely preserve a single book.

We believe what we read in history books with no second thought. We believe what we read in the newspaper. We believe what we hear on the evening news. Why is it so hard to believe in the Bible? I believe the answer to that question is Jesus. If the Bible didn't claim Jesus is the One who is sent from God, then all of mankind would embrace it more readily. Basically, because the Bible says that Jesus is God, it isn't politically correct. It is controversial to some—perhaps to the same people who believe that all roads lead to heaven. Jesus is the dividing line. He is the lightning rod. God is universal and relatively easy to believe in, but Jesus is a different story. The Bible makes no allowances for anything else: Jesus is the only way to heaven.

How Jesus Gets in the Way

The belief that Jesus was not just another great prophet is the entire basis of the Christian faith. Those who argue that Jesus was a great man but not God seem to contradict themselves. If one does not believe that Jesus was who He said He was, you must conclude He was crazy. I would never say that someone is great if they make outlandish, ridiculous claims. People who do that are labeled psychotic, not great.

Jesus said He was God. He said it more than once. In fact, He said it over and over and in no uncertain terms. In John 10:30 Jesus says, "I and My Father are one." That's pretty clear, and it wasn't an insignificant remark made in passing. Jesus was crucified for this claim. He held firm on this until His final breath. To say that Jesus was a great man but not God doesn't make sense to me. If Jesus wasn't God, He was crazy.

And if He wasn't God, the Bible is wrong. And if the Bible is wrong, then everything we believe as Christians is in doubt. But good news, the Bible is not wrong, Jesus is God, and He alone is the only way to heaven. Let's look at the specific passages in the Bible that tell us this.

First, of course, are Jesus' own words in John 14:6. There He tells us forthrightly, "I am the way, the truth, and the life. No one comes to the Father except through Me." That is about as direct as one can be. *No one* gets to heaven except through Jesus. Jesus is the gatekeeper.

So how does one get through Jesus? Again, we need to look no further than what Jesus Himself had to say. In John 6:28 that very question was asked of Him: "What shall we do that we may work the works of God?" They are asking Jesus point-blank, "How do we get to heaven?" His reply, in verse 29 is, "This is the work of God, that you believe in Him whom He sent." That's it.

Jesus could have given an essay on leading a good life. He could have taken the opportunity to repeat the Ten Commandments or the virtues of good, clean living. Instead, He gave a short but to-the-point answer: Believe in the one God sent. He could have said, "Believe in Me," but He chose to honor God. God did the sending. Jesus was simply doing the Father's bidding. Nonetheless, simple belief is all that is required to go to heaven. Do you find that hard to believe? Are you shaking your head? It's true. Belief in Jesus is it. We'll cover this simple truth in a later chapter a bit more extensively, but one needs to look no further than the thief on the cross for a real example. I'll set the stage. Jesus was crucified on a cross between two common criminals. One of the criminals mocked Jesus, saying "If you are the Christ, save Yourself, and us." The other criminal rebuked him and said, "We receive the due reward of our deeds; but this Man has done nothing wrong." Then the thief turned to Jesus and said, "Lord, remember me when You come into Your kingdom."

It is important to note that the thief addressed Jesus as Lord. This is how we know that he indeed believed in Jesus. Jesus affirmed his faith by responding, "Assuredly, I say to you, today you will be with Me in Paradise."[2]

Think about that. Here was a guy who was a criminal. He didn't know Jesus until seconds before his death, yet he went with Jesus to Paradise. It's an amazing example of the only path to heaven. Believe in Jesus as God and you will go to heaven. It's that simple, but it's that narrow. There's no other way. It may not sound logical, fair, or explainable.

"God so loved the world that he gave his one and only Son, that whoever believes in Him shall not perish, but have eternal life (NIV)." That is probably the most quoted most popular passage in Scripture. It's John 3:16. It doesn't say anything about living a good life, helping old ladies across the street, giving a lot of money to charity, or serving on a church committee. It says whoever believes in Jesus will have eternal life, thus going to heaven.

I know that may offend other religions. I know that may offend worldly thinking. It's human nature to believe that God will cut us a break. He knows our hearts, we think. If we've basically been a good person, that's what is important.

Being a good person is a positive thing, but it doesn't have anything to do with getting to heaven. Heaven is reserved for believers in Jesus. Jesus always has and always will be the dividing line. He is the only way to heaven. That may not be politically correct, but it's scripturally correct. Believing otherwise may be hazardous to your eternal health!

CHAPTER 3

BELIEF #2

When We Die, We Become Angels

There are countless books written about angels and the predominant belief among many is that we become angels when we get to heaven. One of my favorite shows of all time featured Michael Landon as an angel who roamed the country doing good deeds. The show was *Highway to Heaven,* and in one of my favorite episodes, Jonathan (Michael Landon) visited his widow and helped her in time of need. It was a great show, and it was really entertaining. But it's biblically inaccurate. As with all the beliefs discussed in this book, the truth is even better!

My own, and certainly informal, survey conducted at my church seminars reveals that the majority of Christians believe they have a guardian angel who was once a human. Most of the time, it's a relative who has passed away. I, myself, have a grandmother who left this world in 1977, and I've often taken comfort in thinking she was watching over me. It's a comforting thought and one that may be true, but my grandmother is not an angel. Let's begin by exploring what angels are and why they're important.

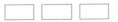

The Bible refers to angels almost 300 times. Angels are one of God's special creations. They were created for a specific purpose, but they are not human. Never have been, never will be. Humans are humans, animals are animals, and angels are angels. To a believer, death is nothing more than relocation. We leave this world and instantly enter the next. There's no lapse in time. The moment we stop breathing physically, we are with the Lord. We know this from 2 Corinthians 5:8. We don't change who we are. We don't become another person, and we don't become angels. We maintain our own identity. We will have our same names and retain our same bodies, albeit far better ones than what we're stuck in presently.

The same is true of angels. They have their own identities. The Bible refers to several angels by their first names. They've been known to appear like humans,[1] but they are 100 percent spirit. The Bible refers to them in Hebrews 1:14 as "ministering spirits." Further, angels are not as special to God as are humans. Angels have more power, greater mobility, and a higher knowledge than do humans, but angels were created to serve us, not the other way around. Paul writes of our worthiness in 1 Corinthians 6:3 and says that we will judge angels. (For this reason, we should not worship angels, although many people do. More on why we shouldn't elevate the stature of angels a bit later.)

What Do Angels Do?

Angels are like God's servants, soldiers, and messengers. We know that God and His army of angels will ultimately do battle against the forces of evil, after which Christ will be crowned king. Angels do God's bidding and serve God in ways that we will never know this side of heaven, but we do know that God uses angels in two specific capacities. First, they help accomplish God's plan on earth, and second, they help guard and serve believers.

The Bible is full of stories of how angels came to the aid of believers. It was the angel Gabriel who was sent by God to inform Mary that she was to give birth to the baby Jesus. Gabriel comforted Mary and reassured her that God would be with her every step of the way. It was an angel that guarded and aided Peter in prison. Angels assisted

Moses when he led the people of Israel through the Red Sea and it was an angel that first appeared to Moses in the burning bush. It was an angel that found water for Abram's wife Sarai, and of course, there was an angel who rescued Shadrach, Meshach, and Abed-Nego from the fiery furnace.

You remember that story from Sunday school perhaps. King Nebuchadnezzar was mad that these three men would not worship the golden image he set up and ordered them to be thrown into the fiery furnace. It is of importance to note that Shadrach, Meshach, and Abed-Nego were completely bound and the furnace was exceedingly hot. In fact, it was so hot that when the king's guards opened the door to the furnace, a flame from the fire killed them instantly. A few moments later, the king noticed not three, but four men, walking in the midst of the fire.

> Angels are used to carry out God's plan on earth, even when we can't figure out what that plan might be.

The fourth, he said, looked like the Son of God. It was an angel the king had seen. That account is one of the Bible's most popular stories and is told in Daniel 3:19-30.

Then there are stories of how God used angels to accomplish His plan on earth. The first biblical account of God using angels is in Genesis 3:24. When Adam and Eve sinned against God, He drove them from the Garden. God placed an angel at the entrance of the Garden of Eden so they could not go back. In Numbers 22:20-35, there is a wonderful story of how God used an angel to get the prophet Balaam to do what God intended. I'd love for you to read the entire story, but in several verses, the angel actually blocked the path that Balaam wanted to travel on. The story really brings to life the words of David in Psalm 34:7: "The angel of the LORD encamps all around those who fear Him, and delivers them," and Psalm 91:11, "He shall give His angels charge over you, to keep you in all your ways."

Indeed angels guide us, remind us, comfort us, inform us, encourage us, warn us, assist us, protect us, and even do harm to us. In 2 Kings 19:35-36, and 2 Samuel 24:15-17, God sent an angel to destroy people, one to punish and one to protect. Angels are used to carry out God's plan on earth, even when we can't figure out what that plan might be.

My Encounters of the Angelic Kind

Those are but just a small few of the stories from the Bible of how angels were used by God. They are simply too numerous to mention them all. There are also countless books written since that recount modern-day stories of angels intervening in the lives of believers. I know of separate instances in my life when I know beyond a shadow of a doubt that angels were present.

The first happened when I was 17. I worked part-time as a home-health aide. My job was to help provide basic care of elderly or physically handicapped people. It was an odd job for a teenager to have, but the hours were good and I met some wonderful people. One reoccurring assignment was to help a gentleman named Mike Parsley. Mike was in his early 30s and had an awesome life. He was married, making good money, and had three great kids. That is, until one night when he had a car accident. I don't recall the details of the accident, but it left him a quadriplegic.

As a result, his wife took the two younger children and left him. Mike and his older boy had to move back into the small government subsidized apartment where his elderly (and quite disabled on their own) parents lived. Despite his seemingly unfortunate circumstances, I don't think I've ever met a happier man in my life. He was always smiling and was reading from the Bible whenever I walked in his door. It was Mike who taught me never to trust the word of man, but to always refer to the Bible for wisdom.

Well, it was nearing Christmas and I decided to do my seasonal good deed. I bought a small fake Christmas tree and a few boxes of trimmings and ornaments for Mike's apartment. With arms full of Christmas cheer, I headed for the back-door entrance to his building. I remember the day like it was yesterday. The rear apartment door was a big steel door that wasn't easy to open even without arms full of boxes. I remember saying out loud as I approached the door, "Lord, help me with this door." At that moment, the door swung open. I hesitated, thinking someone was walking out and opened it from the inside, but that wasn't the case. The big steel door stayed open until I walked through it! To this day, I can't explain it intellectually, but I know it was an angel. Mike told me so.

Jumping ahead to my adult years, I have spoken and written of Mike Parsley often. The world thought I was taking care of him, but really it was the other way around. I have tried numerous times to find him to thank him. Thousands of people have heard me tell stories of him. I've tried every means I know of to trace him, but interestingly, no record of him exists. Don't think for a minute that I haven't begun to wonder whether he was an angel himself. The passage in Hebrews 13:2 is one I've often referred to: "Do not forget to entertain strangers, for by so doing some have unwittingly entertained angels."

The other occurrence that I attribute to an angel happened recently to my daughter, Lauren. It was Sunday night, October 22, 2006. Lauren was driving back to school after dark and took a route I warned her not to take. She wanted to cut a few minutes off her one-hour drive by winding through a back road that was dimly lit and had only a couple residences on it for miles.

At 10:37 PM I got the phone call no parent wants to get. It was a shaken Lauren telling me she had flipped her car. She swerved to avoid an animal and was in pain, disoriented, and couldn't even tell me exactly where she was. Within seconds, my wife and I were en route. We might not have ever seen her Blazer off the side of the road, which had landed on its side and was mangled beyond recognition, if it hadn't been for the emergency lights of the police cars that had beaten us to the scene.

Only then did we realize that several miracles had taken place that night. Somehow Lauren had managed to pull herself up and out of the vehicle as fuel was pouring from the wreckage. The car could have burst into flames at any moment. She had to climb up and out the passenger side and jump down over the burning hot underbelly of the car. Amazingly, there was a single small house directly across the road from the wreckage. She limped her way to the house and thankfully the owner took her in and called the police. She was taken to the hospital, but suffered only a separated shoulder, bruised ribs, and a few minor cuts and scratches.

It was only when we examined the wreck the next day that the extent of the miracle really hit home. The car had flipped several times before crashing roof first into a big oak tree. The impact of the collision with the tree almost severed the car, now resembling the letter "V," in two. The point of impact was right through the place the driver sits. How her head avoided being crushed by the impact is still uncertain, but this much we have concluded. There was a six-inch pocket to the right of the steering wheel where her head must have found refuge. Had she not been in the exact right leaning-forward position, she almost certainly would have been killed or injured badly at best.

We were thankful and knew it had to have been an angel that guided her body into the only spot where she could have avoided the impact, but it wasn't until we went back to the scene of the crash that we knew for sure. Off to the side of the road, next to the oak tree in the brush and debris, we saw something I am certain wasn't there the night before. There, perfectly balancing itself in a sticky bush was an unblemished piece of paper my daughter had drawn on only hours before the crash. She had decorated it with the words, "Life Is Good."

Tears came to our eyes as we thanked the Lord yet again. We naturally saved (and framed) the piece of paper, and we tell everyone we can that angels are among us and life is good! I believe there was an angel with Lauren that night to protect her, but it wasn't someone who once was a human.

God, Not Angels, Provides a Way Out

This might be a good place to interject another, but related, popular belief that is completely misunderstood. I almost gave this belief its own chapter. It is the popular belief that God will not give you more than you can bear. So many people believe this, and many believe it's the sole job of angels to protect us from circumstances getting too much to handle. Believing this, however, may cause some to not trust God when they find themselves in a situation when clearly they can bear no more.

How God's words got twisted and misinterpreted I do not know, but this is what Scripture says in 2 Corinthians 1:8-9:

> We do not want you to be ignorant, brethren, of our trouble which came to us in Asia: that we were burdened beyond measure, above strength, so that we despaired even of life. Yes, we had the sentence of death in ourselves, that we should not trust in ourselves but in God who raises the dead.

Wow. Here was the apostle Paul admitting he felt so burdened, he wanted to die! So what gives? The truth is if it is God's plan for you, you may find yourself in circumstances beyond what you can bear before you find the way out. Scripture never promised you a rose garden, but it does promise an eventual escape route. The Bible assures us in 1 Corinthians 10:13, also written by Paul, that God "will not allow you to be tempted beyond what you are able, but with the temptation will also make the way of escape, that you may be able to bear it."

The point to note is twofold:

1. There may be a period of tremendous burden that pushes you to the edge of despair. This is not God testing or punishing you; it's simply part of God's greater, overall plan. (More on that later.)

2. Angels are just as subject to God's plan as we are, and it's not angels who provide the escape, it is God. Neither angels nor dead relatives can prevent the pain, and they can't bring the relief. That is God's job and His alone!

Raise Your Sights

What's the big deal? What harm is it if we want to believe Aunt

Sally is our guardian angel? After all, Christian bookstores sell a ton of angel paraphernalia. Well, hopefully by now, you've come to believe that the notion of humans becoming angels is biblically incorrect. Besides that, there are two additional reasons why I believe this popular belief is damaging.

The first is, it creates an unnecessary layer between us and God. Why talk to an angel when we can talk directly to the Lord? Why pray to an angel when we can pray directly to the Father? While I am most certainly thankful for angels, especially the ones I've just written about, it is God whom I thank. He sent the angels. The angels didn't do it on their own. They didn't come up with the plan and seek God's permission. It was God's plan and He sent His angels. Creating a layer between us and God creates inevitable distance.

> Appreciate angels for what they are but don't elevate them beyond where they belong. Nothing should occupy the top step except God.

God sent His Son so we can have access to Him directly, and Jesus once said that no one can come to the Father except through Him. Not through the angels—He said through Him.

The second reason why elevating angels is damaging is it is borderline idol worship. The Lord Jesus is who we should praise and worship. It is easy to exalt angels at the expense of Jesus. After all, angels are sexy. It's politically correct to talk about angels. It won't offend anyone to tell of one's experiences with angels, but mention Jesus and it's another story. I know people who readily admit they wear angel jewelry because it is less offensive to nonbelievers. This is precisely my point. Angels often get the credit and glory that should go elsewhere. No master would ever wear the charm of their servant. Angels are God's servants and our master should be God.

Paul wrote about this point blank in Colossians 2:18-19,

> Let no one cheat you of your reward, taking delight in false humility and worship of angels, intruding into those things which he has not seen, vainly puffed up by his fleshly mind,

and not holding fast to the Head, from whom all the body, nourished and knit together by joints and ligaments, grows with the increase that is from God.

Paul knew way back then that angels could become an issue, and I believe it has. That's why it's part of this book. Angels may be politically correct, and sales of angel relics will continue, but make no mistake about it, angels are not to be worshipped. Angels may be a safe topic, and I admit they're very intriguing, but they're a spiritual trap. There are more books in print about angels than about God, and I'm afraid it's easy to get our eyes on the wrong ball. Appreciate angels for what they are but don't elevate them beyond where they belong. Nothing should occupy the top stop except God.

So, if you want to believe your dead Aunt Sally is watching over you, that's your business, but don't do it because you believe she is your guardian angel or because you believe she's got a special in with God. She knows better, and she's pointing you instead to Jesus.

Angels are awesome. I know they're with me and that gives me comfort, but everything comes from God. These words from the apostle Paul say it better and more concisely than I ever could. In Colossians 1:16 he writes,

By Him all things were created that are in heaven and that are on earth, visible and invisible, whether thrones or dominions or principalities or powers. All things were created through Him and for Him.

And that includes angels.

GOD IS NOT A MICROMANAGER • EVERYONE HAS THEIR OWN FREE WILL • THERE AR
ROADS TO HEAVEN • WHEN WE DIE WE BECOME ANGELS • GOD HELPS THOSE WHO HEL
SELVES • GOD WANTS YOU TO BE RICH • CHRISTIANS AREN'T PERFECT, JUST FORGIVEN
RE GOD'S CO-PILOTS • PRAY HARD AND GOD WILL ANSWER • GOD AND SATAN ARE BATTLIN
IT • GOD IS NOT A MICROMANAGER • EVERYONE HAS THEIR OWN FREE WILL • THERE AR
ROADS TO HEAVEN • WHEN WE DIE WE BECOME ANGELS • GOD HELPS THOSE WHO HEI
SELVES • GOD WANTS YOU TO BE RICH • CHRISTIANS AREN'T PERFECT, JUST FORGIVEN
RE GOD'S CO-PILOTS • PRAY HARD AND GOD WILL ANSWER • GOD AND SATAN ARE BATTLIN

CHAPTER 4

BELIEF #3:

God Helps Those
Who Help Themselves

I did a very small and informal survey surrounding this popular belief. I asked ten people at a prayer gathering I attended in my hometown if they believed God helped those who helped themselves. They all said yes, but even more surprising was that eight out of ten said it was a passage from Scripture. The Barna Group did an even bigger study back in 2000. When asked if the Bible teaches that God helps those who help themselves, 53 percent said they agreed, and 22 percent said they somewhat agreed. It may sound logical and harmless, but I hope to prove that it can be damaging and, again, that the truth is a whole lot better!

Let's Talk About Ben Franklin

Where this notion came from is not completely clear, but we do know that it was a favorite saying of Benjamin Franklin. Franklin was an innovative man and he certainly was well educated, but he was no biblical scholar. While he believed in a providential God, Franklin could hardly be called a Christian. He believed Jesus was a great moral teacher but doubted Jesus' divinity. In fact, Franklin is implicated in many of the popular beliefs of which I write. If it sounded reasonable and logical, Franklin supported it. He had little faith in faith.

Here is what Franklin himself said about Christianity: "I have found Christian dogma unintelligible. Early in life I absented myself from Christian assemblies." Franklin's religion was largely intellectual reason. He was a worldly teacher who appealed to the natural human desires to want to be in control. Sadly, more people today follow Franklin's teachings than those of the Bible!

Now, I guess I should point out that Franklin may not have come up with "God helps those who help themselves" entirely by himself. This notion can be traced back to Greek mythology. It originated in one of Aesop's fables, "Hercules and the Waggoner." In that fable, a waggoner was driving a heavy load down a muddy trail and finally became stuck. The Waggoner threw down his whip and knelt to pray to Hercules for help. But Hercules appeared to him and said, "Tut-tut, man, don't sprawl there. Get up and put your shoulder to the wheel. The gods help them that help themselves." So, you see, Franklin just may have borrowed his wisdom from Hercules!

God Will Be Grateful for a Hand, Right?

Regardless of how it originated, the more important questions are whether it is harmful and what the truth is. Let's look at the issue of whether it is harmful to believe that God helps those who help themselves first.

Like all the popular beliefs discussed in this book, it certainly is aligned with worldly wisdom. It basically says that God is more likely to help you if you take action. If you do something about your lot in life, God stands ready and able to help you. If not, don't expect God to come to your rescue. I can't help but recall the Tom Cruise movie *Jerry McGuire*. In that movie, Jerry says one of my favorite lines: "Help me help you." In other words, if you help, then I can help.

It was great drama, but it is not biblical. God rescues us quite a bit, often before we even know we need to do anything, but we'll examine that a bit later. The point I want to explore here is the one about finding more of God's favor through our actions. This is what is damaging. If we can find favor with God, or even elicit more of God's help through the things we do, then our works become the focal point of our relationship with Him. We could never be sure that we have put in enough effort, and how much of our own effort does God require? Does He require 1 percent, 20 percent, 50 percent? Might He require 10 percent on one job and 25 percent on another? It's a question that can be very unsettling.

Does this explain why some people live on easy street and others live in poverty? Is it because those who live on easy street found more of God's favor than those in poverty? Most of humankind believes it. How often do we see someone who is down and out, and our first reaction is that of exhorting them to "do something." It's almost basic instinct to pass judgment on those less fortunate. We exhort a homeless person to "get a job," or tell a beggar to "clean up." We're telling them that God will help them *if* they help themselves first. That's much easier than lending a helping hand ourselves. We rationalize that if we helped them, it would only make things worse. They might never learn the lesson of helping themselves.

We are a works society and are even defined by what we do for a living. A president of a large corporation is more important than a cobbler.[1] We introduce ourselves by profession. "That's Sally, she's a bank teller." "That's Bob, he drives a truck." "Over there is Mitch, he builds houses." Our identity is intertwined with what we do. It's no wonder we believe our works will determine God's blessings. The more we do, the more we'll get. It may be a law of the land, but it's not God's law.

God's law says just the opposite. Speaking of God's choosing whom He will, the apostle Paul writes in Romans 11:6, "If by grace, then it is no longer of works; otherwise grace is no longer grace. But if it is of works, it is no longer grace; otherwise work is no longer work." It can't be both. It has to be one or the other. Grace is unmerited favor. It means there's nothing we did or can do to earn it. It is a free gift. Works says, the more we do, the more we get. They are mutually exclusive, and the Bible is completely clear that we are saved by grace, as Ephesians 2:8 says: "By grace you have been saved through faith, and that is not of yourselves, it is the gift of God, not through works, lest anyone should boast." We gain favor through grace, not through works. It is a gift of God and there is absolutely nothing we can do to precipitate it, otherwise it wouldn't be a free gift. Grace is a gift and that's precisely why we should fall on our knees in thankfulness at the very thought of it.

Can We Finish God's Job?

Now some might say that we are saved by grace, but once we become saved, then there are things we must do to remain in God's favor. Well, this is equally false. It's amazing to me that so many Christians readily believe that we are saved through no effort of our own, but once saved, the rules change.

I had a debate one time with an elder from a very large church who argued this point with me. He acknowledged that we indeed are saved by grace, but once saved, he rattled off a laundry list of works. On his list were attending church regularly, praying multiple times each day and night, tithing a minimum of 10 percent of your income, giving to the needy, ministering to the sick and elderly, going on mission trips to spread the word of God, being an example to those not saved, reading from the Bible daily, and conducting family Bible studies, just to name a few.

While I certainly cannot and would not argue that those are all good things to do, they are not conditions of grace. Doing them will not gain or lose favor with God. We do them because we want to do them, not because it is a Christian requirement. Grace does not come with a set of conditions. To say, or believe, that the rules change once you're saved is tantamount to saying that the work of the cross was not sufficient. The work of the cross is the only work that we need. Paul writes in Galatians 2:21, "I do not set aside the grace of God; for if righteousness comes through the law [works], then Christ died in vain." We are righteous in God's eyes not because of the things we do, but because of *who* we are.

I'll write more about that in a later chapter, but suffice it to say that the work of the cross is the only work in which we should boast. This is written most plainly in Galatians 6:14, "God forbid that I should boast except in the cross of our Lord Jesus Christ, by whom the world has been crucified to me, and I to the world." Worldly beliefs are not important. The Word of God is what really matters! The cross was a complete work. That is exactly what Paul meant when he wrote in Acts 17:25 that God did not need human hands. The truth—and this one is leaps and bounds better than popular belief—is that God does not need us for one single thing! God uses us. God likes to involve us. God allows us to participate in His plan. God even lets us feel important at times. But He doesn't need us. We need Him. God will never say, "Help me help you." What He might say is, "Have faith that I will help you."

> To borrow from another movie, we're already wearing our ruby slippers! Our job is simply to trust Him.

The truth is God does help us. It's just that His help is not conditional. He wants us to need Him and have faith that He will always guide us through any problems we might encounter. If we're focused on doing, it's harder to stay focused on trusting. I like to say that we're either trying or trusting. If we're trying out of our own self-effort, then we're not trusting. If we're trusting, there's no need to try and please God through self-effort. We can rest in knowing we already please Him and that His help is better than our help. To borrow from another movie, we're already wearing our ruby slippers! Our job is to simply trust Him.

The problem is, we think of ourselves as self-sufficient. We're taught that needing is a form of weakness. This flies, however, in the face of Scripture that says the opposite. In 2 Corinthians 3:4-5, Paul writes, "We have such trust through Christ toward God. Not that we are sufficient to think of anything as being from ourselves, but our sufficiency is from God." God is sufficient. God will help us so that we don't need to help ourselves. We trust; God does the helping.

Strength Comes from Waiting

In direct contrast with the notion of God helping if we help first, Scripture paints a different picture. Scripture says that God does indeed help, but only if we "wait." Waiting is not working. It's not helping, but rather trusting. When we fully wait on God and trust His help, it's amazing how much more aware we become of the ways He does help. God's help often comes in ways we're not expecting, thus making us feel like He hadn't helped us at all. God allows us to feel His help in different ways. So we feel if we don't help ourselves, no one will help. This, of course, promotes the feeling of self-sufficiency, and less trusting. That's why it's crucial we know, so we can recognize the ways in which we experience God's help. Let's look at the three kinds of help we get from God.

The three kinds of help we get from God can be best described (of course) by using Scripture. Turn to Isaiah 40:31. This is a pretty well-known passage. It reads, "Those who wait on the LORD shall renew their strength; they shall mount up with wings like eagles, they shall run and not be weary, they shall walk and not faint." Notice the pivotal word in that passage, "wait." *Those who wait, not those who do, can expect God's help.*

Let's break Isaiah 40:31 down a bit further. The first part says that it is those who wait on the Lord that will find strength. Waiting is like trusting. It is very passive. It doesn't mean that we will sit in a chair until God calls us home—it simply means that we count on Him to help, not ourselves. We should put our faith in Him, not humankind. If we count on God, He might help us by mounting us up with wings like eagles. This is what we hope happens all the time. This is where God swoops in and transforms our circumstances. It is where God performs a miracle. God rescues us from our circumstances.

Mounting up with wings as eagles is what we pray when we find ourselves backed into a corner. It's when we're the most vulnerable. It's when we know we can't do anything ourselves and desperately need God's intervention. The truth is, this describes our situation all the time, only we often don't realize it. Both you and I have experienced

God's miraculous intervention. We've seen or at least heard of times when against all odds, someone was cured of cancer. We all know of stories of amazing rescue that God has performed. It's too bad we need miraculous intervention for us to realize our total dependency on God. Nonetheless, this is one way God chooses to help.

The second way is for God to allow us to run and not grow weary. God gives us the ability to run. Running certainly means we're doing something, but our strength comes directly from God. This is where God allows us to participate in transforming our circumstances. This may be a time when cancer doesn't miraculously disappear, but it goes into remission after exhausting rounds of chemotherapy and treatment. This kind of help is certainly less desirable than mounting up with wings like eagles, but we're grateful nonetheless.

Now you may be thinking that this sounds an awful lot like "God helps those who help themselves." Well, not intentionally. The difference lies in who is getting the credit and who is the source of your strength. If the source of your strength is yourself, and you get the credit, then it's completely wrong. You think you're helping yourself and that is buying into the false popular belief. If you recognize God as the source and give Him the credit, there's no helping involved. It's all Him. It's divine empowerment, which incidentally, is the only kind of empowerment there is.

The final kind of help we can expect from God is to walk and not faint. We walk, or maybe even limp, through our situation. This is where circumstances don't change. God doesn't swoop in, nor does He grant us the power to change them. He simply allows us to endure. We grit our teeth and bear the circumstances, as painful as that might be. This, to us, is the least desirable kind of help. It's much preferable to experience miracles. It's easy to think that we didn't get any help from God when our circumstances don't change. In fact, things may get worse.

This doesn't mean God isn't with us or helping. Enduring is a form of help. There's a reason for everything that happens, even if we don't ever find out what that reason is. We simply must keep our eye on God. Trust Him for your strength. Trust that He will not allow you to faint. This doesn't mean things will go the way you may want them to go, but it's the way God wants them to go.

A biblical passage that comforts me during trying times is 2 Corinthians 12:7-10:

> Lest I should be exalted above measure by the abundance of the revelations, a thorn in the flesh was given to me, a messenger of Satan to buffet me, lest I be exalted above measure. Concerning this thing I pleaded with the Lord three times that it might depart from me. And He said to me, "My grace is sufficient for you, for My strength is made perfect in weakness." Therefore most gladly I will rather boast in my infirmities, that the Power of Christ may rest upon me. Therefore I take pleasure in infirmities, in reproaches, in needs, in persecutions, in distresses, for Christ's sake. For when I am weak, then I am strong.

We are strong when we completely trust in the Lord. Humanly that appears as weakness, but to God, it is ultimate strength.

We may pray that God mounts us up on His shoulders, but He may choose another path for us. God chooses how He helps. He determines the whens and the wheres, we bow in humble thankfulness. It's all to promote grace and thanksgiving. "All things are for your sakes, that grace, having spread through the many, may cause thanksgiving to abound to the glory of God." This is from 2 Corinthians 4:15 and it says everything in a few words that I've been trying to say for pages. Grace, which is the opposite of works, causes thanksgiving, and everything that happens is for the glory of God.

Lay down your works and get off the worldly treadmill. Grace is a much stronger position than always trying to gain what you already possess. You cannot find any more favor from God than what you already have. The sooner we realize and accept our total dependency on God, the sooner we will find true peace and rest. Be worldly weak and you will be spiritually strong. God doesn't help those who help themselves, only those who trust Him to do so.

GOD IS NOT A MICROMANAGER • EVERYONE HAS THEIR OWN FREE WILL • THERE AR
ROADS TO HEAVEN • WHEN WE DIE WE BECOME ANGELS • GOD HELPS THOSE WHO HEL
SELVES • GOD WANTS YOU TO BE RICH • CHRISTIANS AREN'T PERFECT, JUST FORGIVEN
RE GOD'S CO-PILOTS • PRAY HARD AND GOD WILL ANSWER • GOD AND SATAN ARE BATTLIN
T • GOD IS NOT A MICROMANAGER • EVERYONE HAS THEIR OWN FREE WILL • THERE AR
ROADS TO HEAVEN • WHEN WE DIE WE BECOME ANGELS • GOD HELPS THOSE WHO HEL
SELVES • GOD WANTS YOU TO BE RICH • CHRISTIANS AREN'T PERFECT, JUST FORGIVEN
RE GOD'S CO-PILOTS • PRAY HARD AND GOD WILL ANSWER • GOD AND SATAN ARE B

CHAPTER 5

BELIEF #4

God Wants You to Be Rich

Why wouldn't God want us to be rich? God wants all His children to partake in the material things of this world, right? This popular belief may sound awfully good to our human senses, but as with all of the popular beliefs in this book, it simply isn't biblical. (As Martin Luther is said to have written, "They gave our Master a crown of thorns—why do we hope for a crown of roses?")

Perhaps it is rooted in another popular belief that isn't true that God created everyone equal. We may have equal rights as citizens of planet Earth. We're all important. We're all created by God in His image, but we're not equal. I ran across this notion many years ago in the form of popular quote: "What you are is God's gift to you, what you make of yourself is your gift to God." This implies that we are all equal lumps of clay and it's up to us to make something of our lives.

I like the idea. I think it's good to make something of our lives, but we all don't start out equal. Some might argue that merely being born in America is a huge advantage, especially in the wealth-building area, than being born in a poorer country. Indeed God has us where He wants us and gives us separate (but not equal) talents and abilities to work together for His good.

More on that in an upcoming chapter, but wherever the idea came from that God wants us to be rich, it has gained steam in recent years.

There are countless ministries, and even more books, across the country that claim God does want you to be unequivocally and filthy rich. Many claim that all you need to do is "name it and claim it." It even has a name. It's called the "Prosperity Gospel."

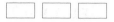

I was first introduced to the concept in the early 1980s. Fresh out of college, I was all about making money. My family didn't have much money, so I was bound and determined to make millions. A friend of our family introduced me to Amway, and I just knew I was on my way. Amway, at least back then, was full-throttle prosperity teaching. All you had to do was tell God what you want, and if you have enough faith, it can be yours. In essence, you can speak what you want into existence. "Name it, claim it."

It resonated with me, as it did with countless others who attended Amway rallies all across the country. Speaker after speaker recited the same message. God wants everyone to have health and wealth, and it was up to me to make sure I received my fair-share slice of the abundance pie. I even recall one speaker saying that if we didn't become wealthy, we were letting God down! I was given a book by Paul Zane Pilzer aptly titled *God Wants You to Be Rich*, which is not a bad book, but it is much more about economics than it is about godly teaching.

> They are clearly striking a chord, but I contend the chord they are striking is nothing more than human vanity.

I was fully indoctrinated into believing wealth was my right as a Christian. I spent the better part of the '80s and '90s chasing material wealth. I had my share of successes, but I never became wealthy. I often felt like a miserable failure in God's eyes because I hadn't struck gold. I must not have had enough faith. I recall many chats, and even a few letters, to God rededicating myself to Him and promising that I would do better. Despite my pleas and promises, I never became filthy rich.

It's important to note that I certainly don't fault Amway for the fact I didn't become Bill Gates. I was only involved a couple of years on a part-time basis at best. And I also don't blame them for inventing the "Prosperity Gospel." Although they might have helped the cause, prosperity teachings were around long before Amway and are flourishing today more than ever. All you need to do is turn on your TV or walk into the religious section of your local bookstore to know that this thinking is alive and well. Of the four biggest megachurches in the country, three are heavy on prosperity teachings.* It's hard to argue with their success. They are clearly striking a chord, but I contend the chord they are striking is nothing more than human vanity, and that the notion that God wants all His children to be healthy and wealthy is not only *not* biblical, but damaging to a true relationship with God. Let's first look at whether it is biblical or not.

Prosperity You Can't Even Imagine

Clearly there are references in Scripture to abundance and prosperity. In 3 John 2, John begins by saying, "Beloved, I pray that you may prosper in all things and be in health, just as your soul prospers." Proponents of prosperity teaching frequently point to that verse (among others, of course) to prove their case. However, most theologians agree that John was doing nothing more than greeting a friend with well wishes. It is one thing for us to wish and want good things to happen to each other; it is a completely different thing to say that God wants the same things.

Some also point to John 10:10 and quote the words of Jesus, "I have come that they may have life, and that they may have it more abundantly." The whole argument hinges on the definition of the word *abundance.* Proponents loosely twist that text into meaning material wealth. I say that Jesus is speaking on spiritual abundance, not money. Jesus made it very clear that our riches were not in this physical world, but rather in the spiritual realm. Look at Matthew 6:19-20:

---

* Joel Osteen's Lakewood in Houston, T.D. Jakes' Potter's House in Dallas, and Creflo Dollar's World Changers outside of Atlanta.

> Do not lay up for yourselves treasures on earth, where moth
> and rust destroy and where thieves break in and steal; but
> lay up for yourselves treasures in heaven, where neither moth
> nor rust destroys and where thieves do not break in and
> steal.

These are also words of Jesus, and He was clearly not speaking of money. Thieves steal money all the time. The treasures Jesus was referring to are spiritual. When the Bible refers to prosperity and abundance, it is speaking of the treasure that awaits all believers in heaven. Our wealth is spiritual, not physical.

In fact, Jesus warned repeatedly about the dangers of gaining too much physical wealth. In Matthew 19:21 He said, "If you want to be perfect, go, sell what you have and give it to the poor, and you will have treasure in heaven; and come follow Me." If God wanted you to have physical wealth, why would Jesus tell anyone to sell everything and give it to the poor? This text is the story of the rich young ruler who already had great riches, but he didn't have the real treasure of a relationship with God. Later in Matthew 19:24, Jesus says, "It is easier for a camel to go through the eye of a needle than for a rich man to enter the kingdom of God." This is an odd thing to say if God wants everyone to be rich. According to Jesus, money will only hinder your relationship with God, not strengthen it. Money makes you more self-reliant. It makes us feel less dependent on God. It makes us feel prideful and more important.

The truth is, money is a wedge between us and God. Jesus said in Matthew 6:24 that "no one can serve two masters," and that "you cannot serve God and mammon." (*Mammon* is Greek for money.) Paul later wrote in 1 Timothy 6:10 that the love for money is the root of all kinds of evil. Paul didn't say money was evil, but rather the love or quest for money was the root of all varieties of evil. As believers, we are already wealthy, but our treasure is in following Jesus. Our treasure is awaiting us in heaven. This is precisely what Jesus indicated in John 15:18-19:

If the world hates you, you know that it hated Me before it
hated you. If you were of the world, the world would love its
own. Yet because you are not of the world, but I chose you
out of the world, therefore the world hates you.

Worldly treasures are not promised us. What's promised us are treasures in heaven and that is much better anyway.

A Better Plan for Riches

With all that said, I have to tell you of the time a woman came up
to me after one of my presentations and asked a very good question.
She said that I answered her question on whether God wanted us to
be rich, but did God want us to be poor instead? It made me rethink
how I was teaching this truth. It's not that God doesn't want us to
be rich. After all, there are many great believers who are doing awesome things who are very well off. God just doesn't want us to pursue
money. God doesn't dislike a believer who has money any more than
He doesn't like a believer who doesn't have money.

Some of us may be dirt-poor. Some may be rich. It's simply a matter
of what God has planned for each of us. Riches aren't a Christian
right, and poverty isn't a Christian badge of honor. It's all a matter of
God's purpose for us individually. No matter how much we may want
riches, we can't "name it and claim it." It may be God's will for us
to be rich, and it may be His will for us to live in a box. The believer
who lives in a box under a highway is just as rich (spiritually) as the
person who lives in a mansion. They may not have the money, but
their heavenly bank account is equal. One believer is no more or less
in God's eyes than the other.

Thirsting after money and letting money rule you is what is bad.
As worldly bank accounts grow, it is all too human for our heads to
grow as well. This is how money and the Prosperity Gospel can be
bad. We get to thinking that God is at our service. If we name it and
claim it and have enough faith, He is standing willing and ready to
grant our wishes. It's almost as if God was a divine vending machine.

Drop enough faith into the machine and He'll deliver what you want. I'll address this more in a later chapter concerning prayer, but that is not how God operates. Man doesn't affect God.

All the naming and claiming won't do a thing if it's not in His plan for our life. We know what we want, but He knows what we need and how everything fits into His plans. That may include being healthy and wealthy, it may not. If we believe that it's our right to be healthy and wealthy, and then we're not, it could drive us away from God. We may begin to think God doesn't love us as much as our wealthy neighbor or that we've done something to make God mad. We simply must understand that God has a plan for each of us and it may or may not always be what we think we want.

I am living proof of this. Allow me to share a bit of my life story. I was born in blue-collar Allentown, Pennsylvania. When I was three years old, my mother and father divorced, and I grew up, as too many kids do, without a dad. My mother had to go back to work and worked the night shift at Howard Johnson's as a bookkeeper. My grandparents moved in with us, and my grandmother looked after my sister and me when my mom went to work. Needless to say, there wasn't a lot of leftover money at the end of the month.

I can remember some pretty nasty arguments between my mother and grandmother, all of them over money. When things got a little too intense, I took refuge behind the aluminum shed in our backyard. It was my quiet place, a place where I went hundreds of times. Sometimes I went there to escape, sometimes to play, sometimes to hide, but mostly to pray. The prayer that dominated my childhood went something like this: "Dear Lord, please give us money so Mom and Gam (the nickname we gave to my grandmother) will stop fighting. When I get older, Lord, please give me lots of money. I don't care how it happens; I just want to be rich!"

Well, let's jump ahead to my thirteenth birthday. That year, my mother remarried, and the gentleman she married elected to adopt my sister and me. This is a deed I've come to appreciate more deeply now that I've got teenagers of my own. I humbly concede that I found the patience and strength to endure three strong-willed children through their teenage years only due to remembering the sweet years that preceded them. The man my mother married had been a bachelor his entire life, and in one afternoon, he had two teenagers!

Nevertheless, as with adoptions, I was issued a new birth certificate bearing his last name. His last name was Rich—so overnight, I became Rich.

It wasn't until years later that the irony of my childhood prayers hit me. I joke that apparently, I wasn't specific enough in my prayers. I prayed for fortune, but became rich in an entirely different way. Money was not in God's plan, but a father was.

Focusing on Our Source

I've made a good living, but in no way am I wealthy. If I still believed that it was my right as a Christian to be rich, I'd be very disillusioned by now. Thankfully, I know that God's ideas and plans are always better than any I might come up with on my own. The truth, as I've stated before, is always better than popular belief, and it's that God is in control of our destiny. God is the only source of riches. If God's plan includes riches, be thankful for your undeserved bounty. If God's plan includes poverty, be thankful that money can't buy happiness, much less a relationship with Him. If God's plan includes health, praise Him with a dozen push-ups. If God's plan includes infirmity, praise Him with thought and song. You get the picture. Real peace and security comes from praising God for whatever lot in life is assigned us, not how much is in our bank accounts or what stocks we own. Real prosperity is awaiting us in heaven.

A couple of my favorite verses recap what I am saying. Paul writes that we should be thankful no matter what our lot in life because of the hope of future riches. In Ephesians 1:18 he writes of "the eyes of your understanding being enlightened; that you may know what is the hope of His calling, what are the riches of the glory of His inheritance in the saints." Further in Ephesians 2:7, Paul writes again of God's purpose "that in the ages to come he might show the exceeding riches of His grace in His kindness toward us in Christ Jesus." This is a particularly crucial verse because it says that one day we will see the extent of God's grace in our lives. It's hard to see grace at work every day in the midst of our daily trials and tribulations, but one day, we will realize just how rich we've always been in Christ.

I'll close this chapter with a story that illustrates our fortune in heaven, the story of a man who has always had misfortune in his life. His wife left him. He wasn't in good health, and he had very little money. Most people felt sorry for him, but no one felt more sorry for him than he did himself. He wallowed in his misery. One day he received an overnight delivery of a note that would change his life. The note told of a distant relative who had felt sorry for him. This relative was very wealthy and had left him sole possession of his entire estate which included several houses, many cars, and thousands of acreage. He was no longer poor!

> Whatever you have right now, whether it is pennies or millions, it pales in comparison with what awaits you.

On the man's way to claim his inheritance, it began to rain. Not just a little rain, but a brutal storm. His car broke down in the middle of nowhere and he didn't have a nickel in his pocket, and even if he had, the closest town was at least 30 miles away. He was distraught. He sat there feeling sorry for himself. He was unable to move. He couldn't believe that this could happen to him. After a few days, soaked and chilled to the core, days without food, he died on the side of the road, alone. When he was finally found, a few acquaintances laid him to rest without much fanfare and without knowing of the inheritance he had received just days before. His tombstone read, "Here lies an ordinary man who had a hard life."

Many of you reading this book often feel like an ordinary person who has had their share of hardship. We all have. But the question that this story begs us to ask is this: Did the man in the story die rich or poor? Some might say rich, and some might argue poor. The answer depends on how you look at life and whether you believe riches are the sum of what you have in your pocket right this very moment, or whether riches include all your assets, holdings, and hidden bank accounts. We have an inheritance awaiting us, just like this man did. It doesn't matter what we have in our pockets or our bank accounts right now. We are rich because of what we have in Christ Jesus. We're rich because of who we are. Some of us may have more material wealth here on earth than some others, but we all have the same inheritance. We're all the same in heaven!

Money, and sometimes, as with the man in my story, lack of money, make this hard to see. We only see what we know we can see. We can't see what awaits us in heaven, but a huge inheritance is there nonetheless. So for the time being, for richer or poorer, in sickness or in health, find peace in knowing God wants you to have exactly what you have. That's why you have it. But whatever you have right now, whether it is pennies or millions, it pales in comparison with what awaits you. God may not want you to have money, cars, stocks, or anything of this world, but you have abundant treasures in heaven. So, I guess God does want you to be rich—He just wants to give it to you face-to-face!

IT • GOD IS NOT A MICROMANAGER • EVERYONE HAS THEIR OWN FREE WILL • THERE AR
ROADS TO HEAVEN • WHEN WE DIE WE BECOME ANGELS • GOD HELPS THOSE WHO HEL
SELVES • GOD WANTS YOU TO BE RICH • CHRISTIANS AREN'T PERFECT, JUST FORGIVEN
RE GOD'S CO-PILOTS • PRAY HARD AND GOD WILL ANSWER • GOD AND SATAN ARE BATTLIN
T • GOD IS NOT A MICROMANAGER • EVERYONE HAS THEIR OWN FREE WILL • THERE AR
ROADS TO HEAVEN • WHEN WE D   NGELS • GOD HELPS THOSE WHO HEL
SELVES • GOD WANTS YOU TO BE RICH • CHRISTIANS AREN'T PERFECT, JUST FORGIVEN
            PRAY HARD AND GOD WILL ANSWER • GOD

CHAPTER 6

BELIEF #5

Christians Aren't Perfect, Just Forgiven

O ne of the fastest growing crimes in the twenty-first century is identity theft. Although it is considered a nonviolent crime, it is every bit as harmful in its way, and its effects can last as long as any violent encounter. We work our entire lives creating our identity, and to have it taken away from us can be devastating. I've known people who've been forced into bankruptcy because someone stole their identity. It is not unusual for people who've been victims of identity theft to lose perspective on their real identity.

Identity theft is tragic, but despite its growth, it still affects a rather small percentage of the population. That pales in comparison to the identity theft that has taken place when it comes to knowing who we are in Christ. According to research by the Barna Group, three out of four adults believe it is possible for someone to become holy, yet only 50 percent say they know someone who they consider holy. But catch this—only 21 percent say they consider themselves to be holy.

Those numbers are for the general population. One would think that the numbers would rise substantially if the questions were asked exclusively of born-again Christians. Well, they were, and the results were pretty close. Among believers, 76 percent say it is certainly possible to become holy, but only 55 percent know someone who is.

And only 29 percent say they are holy! That's only slightly higher than the general national norm. Think about that for a second—less than three out of ten Christians see themselves as holy. That's a *real* identity crisis.

You've probably seen a bumper sticker somewhere that echoes this crisis: "Christians aren't perfect, just forgiven." Most believers believe they are nothing more than sinners who've found mercy from God. This is no mystery, because there isn't a Sunday that goes by somewhere in America that a preacher doesn't remind their congregation that they are horribly wretched sinners. I've personally left many a worship service where I not only didn't feel holy, I didn't feel worthy of God's love.

In fact, many nonchurchgoers don't attend a service for this very reason. They don't feel like they deserve to be there. Church, for many, has become the spiritual equivalent to our judicial system. Church convicts us of our sins, informs us of our punishment, and sends us home on house arrest to try to do better and report back in one week. In law enforcement, there is something called the cycle of violence. It's where someone never completely breaks free of their habits and past behavior. Offenders often are on a perpetual cycle of criminal thought and activity. In the Christian world, this is called a cycle of bondage. Most Christians never break free of seeing themselves the way they were, not how they *are!*

"Born Again"—A Label or a Reality?

I've heard people say that Christians are mere sinners who've been saved. In keeping with my penchant to argue crucial but ignored points of theology, part of that is true, and part is untrue. We've been saved by the work of the cross, certainly, but we are no longer mere sinners. That was our former identity, not our current one. Let me illustrate. When someone gets married, they take on a new identity. A woman actually changes her name legally to reflect her new identity. The man, although he doesn't change his name, also is no longer a single, unattached person. They are identified as a married couple. We don't say that they are single people who've been married. We say they're married. That's now who they are.

As believers, we are the bride of Christ. We are no longer who we were. We have become one with the Lord. This shouldn't be that hard to grasp. Everyone is familiar with the moniker *born-again.* Many Christians include this as a precursor to their identity. We're often called "born again Christians." Have you stopped for a moment and pondered what that actually means? Is it just a phrase? What does it mean to become born again? It's a good question and one every believer needs to be clear about.

Being born again is not just a symbolic tag placed on believers. It is an actual event. It is often misunderstood, just as it was back in the day of Jesus. Look at the passages in John 3 when Jesus explained being born again in detail to a man named Nicodemus. In verses 3 through 7,

> Jesus answered and said to him, "Most assuredly, I say to you, unless one is born again, he cannot see the kingdom of God." Nicodemus said to Him, "How can a man be born when he is old? Can he enter a second time into his mother's womb and be born?" Jesus answered, "Most assuredly, I say to you, unless one is born of water and the Spirit, he cannot enter the kingdom of God. That which is born of the flesh is flesh, and that which is born of the Spirit is spirit. Do not marvel that I said to you, You must be born again."

Here Jesus is clearly explaining that being born again is an actual occurrence. Being born of the flesh is different from being born of the Spirit. They are separate experiences. You can only be born once physically, but if you want to enter the kingdom of God, you must be born again spiritually.

But many would argue that this is merely figurative. Many might say that being born again simply means to believe in Jesus, as Jesus

Himself explained further down in John 3, in verse 16. If that is true, why use the term *born again?* That term just confuses people, as it did Nicodemus. I propose that Jesus used the term because it means more than believing. It's an event in the life of every believer.

Which of the following statements is true? Do you believe in Jesus and then become born again, or are you born again and then believe in Jesus? It seems like an inconsequential chicken-or-the-egg question, but it's incredibly important. Many might argue we have faith first, but I say we must become born again first. You cannot have faith if you are not born again of the Spirit. It's a life-changing, identity-changing event.

Paul refers to being born again in even stronger words. Paul calls it a spiritual circumcision. In Colossians 2:11, he writes, "In Him you were also circumcised with the circumcision made without hands, by putting off the body of the sins of the flesh, by the circumcision of Christ." We can't perform our own circumcision. It's more than just a proclamation of faith—it's a surgery performed without human hands. It's an event performed by Christ.

Identity Switch

So what's the implication here? Aren't we still sinners who've been forgiven? The answer is a resounding *no.* We're a new creation in Christ. The person we were before no longer exists. Our new identity is wrapped up in Christ. That's the purpose and the reason for being born again. It's a new birth, and as believers, we are new creatures. That's exactly what the Bible says in 2 Corinthians 5:17: "If anyone is in Christ, he is a new creation; old things have passed away; behold, all things have become new." We're not new and improved versions of our old sinful self—we are a new creation. Our old self has passed away and our new life is in Christ.[1] Our new identity is "in Christ," and we are perfect. After all, how much more perfect can we become than when we're in Christ? When God looks at us, He sees the image of His Son, and that image is perfect.

I like to ask a question in my seminars, a question I borrowed from my mentor, Glenna Salsbury. It's a true–false question: Only perfect people go to heaven—true or false? The answer is, of course, *true!* Only perfect people are in heaven, and thankfully as new creatures in Christ, we are perfect! This life-changing truth is not grasped by the vast majority of believers, as evidenced by the Barna research. We're not sinners anymore if we've been born again.

The strongest and most powerful passage in Scripture to remember is found in 1 Corinthians 6:9-11. It's one I carried around with me for several years as I was struggling with understanding my new identity. Paul writes,

> Do you not know that the unrighteous will not inherit the kingdom of God? Do not be deceived. Neither fornicators, nor idolaters, nor adulterers, nor homosexuals, nor sodomites, nor thieves, nor covetous, nor drunkards, nor revilers, nor extortioners will inherit the kingdom of God. And such *were* some of you. But you were washed, but you were sanctified, but you were justified in the name of the Lord Jesus and by the Spirit of our God.

Isn't that wonderful? Paul is saying that only perfect people go to heaven, but as new creatures, washed by the blood shed by Jesus on the cross, we've been justified and sanctified. We may have been sinners, but that's not who we are anymore.

But you may be thinking, *I still see myself sinning.* You still sin on a daily basis, and you're wondering how that is perfect in God's eyes. It's a valid question, but it's far from original. Paul had the same dilemma. In Romans 7:18-20, Paul struggles with the issue:

> I know that in me (that is, in my flesh) nothing good dwells; for to will is present with me, but how to perform what is good I do not find. For the good that I will to do, I do not do; but the evil I will not to do, that I practice. Now if I do what I will not to do, it is no longer I who do it, but sin that dwells in me.

Paul is a stickler for semantics for the cause of truth when he makes the distinction between himself and his flesh. He says that he wants to do good because that is his new identity, but he finds his flesh still engaged in sin. His flesh does what he doesn't want it to do. That all sounds like doublespeak, but Paul clears it up by saying that he is not doing the sin. Sin stills dwells in his flesh, but *he* is not his flesh.

Who Is the "You" God Knows?

I know this is a tough one to wrap our heads around. It's hard for us to separate our flesh (which is not us) from our spirit (which *is* us)—but it's not hard for God. God sees us in His image and His image is spirit. Though Paul struggled with this truth like all of us, he eventually cleared it all up in Romans 8:5-9:

> Those who live according to the flesh set their minds on the things of the flesh, but those who live according to the Spirit, the things of the Spirit. For to be carnally minded is death, but to be spiritually minded is life and peace. Because the carnal mind is enmity against God; for it is not subject to the law of God, nor indeed can be. So then, those who are in the flesh cannot please God. But you are not in the flesh but in the Spirit, if indeed the Spirit of God dwells in you. Now, if anyone does not have the Spirit of Christ, he is not His.

Let's break those verses down because they contain so much great stuff. First, Paul again makes the distinction between flesh and spirit. Flesh sets its mind on things of the flesh, which are things that make the flesh feel good. Pride, status, money, lust, control, power, sex, vanity, and material possessions are but a few of the worldly things that make the flesh feel good.

However, Paul then writes that if we're ruled by the flesh (in essence by not being born again), we cannot please God and it will lead to death. Then comes the most important word in those verses, *but*. He writes, "But you are not in the flesh but in the Spirit." All believers are "in the Spirit." All believers are "in Christ." All believers are a new creation. All believers are not their flesh. All believers are perfect. All believers have eternal life. All believers will go heaven. How's that for definitiveness?

Now don't be fooled, our flesh is going to continue to sin—but thankfully, our identity is not our flesh. We are not the body we are stuck in here on earth, so regardless of the sin our flesh may still engage in; we are still perfect in God's eyes. That's precisely why we will never die. Think about it. The famous passage of John 3:16 is confusing to many for that very statement. Doesn't everyone die eventually? The answer is *yes* and *no*. Our flesh will die, but we will not. We are not our flesh. We are spirit!

Veiled Perfection

Perfection is tough to grasp, especially while we're still on earth. We see our flesh sin. We experience sin every day. It's easy to feel overwhelmed, but ponder this question for a moment. How many of your sins were forgiven when Jesus died for you on the cross? Did He die for just some of them or all of them? Did He die for just the big ones or for the little ones too? The answer is, of course, for all of them.

I was explaining this truth to a friend one day and my friend threw what he thought was a real monkey wrench in my argument. He said, "Sure, Christ died for my sins, and we're forgiven for the sins we've committed, but we must keep asking for forgiveness if we keep sinning from that point forward." It's a classic misunderstanding of identity, and my friend is not alone. Because many Christians do not understand the identity issue, they mistakenly believe they must specifically ask for forgiveness for any sins they commit after they become saved.

> He's forgiven sins you don't know about, sins you would never imagine committing, and ones you aren't even aware of.

A Catholic friend of the family virtually said those words when she admitted to my wife she hadn't been to confession in a while and feared what might happen if she died before she was able to formally repent. She is unfortunately in bondage. She's a believer, and she's perfect in God's eyes, but she doesn't know who she is.

For anyone reading this book who empathizes with our friend, let me ask one more question that hopefully will help you dig out of bondage. At the time Jesus died on the cross, how many of your sins were future sins? The obvious answer is, they were all future sins. Jesus died, and paid the price, for all the sins you may commit in the future. He knew them then. You can't surprise Him with a sin He didn't see coming. He's forgiven sins you don't know about, sins you would never imagine committing, and ones you aren't even aware of. Sure, you'll repent whenever you do commit a sin, but it's already been forgiven. You repent because sinning is against your identity. You feel bad and guilty because it isn't who you are. If your identity were still "sinner," you wouldn't feel bad about it. Remorse is the way you can tell it's contrary to who you are. People who are not believers still have the identity they were born with. Therefore, they don't feel the guilt, regret, and remorse that believers feel. Sin comes natural to them because it's who they are.

A good friend and colleague, Steve McVey, who incidentally wrote some of my favorite books on the subject of identity, explains it this way.[2] A believer is perfect because of who they are in Christ, even though their flesh may still sin. He calls it their "flesh pattern." Someone might be a perfect saint but have a gambling flesh pattern, or a drinking flesh pattern. The flesh will never be perfect this side of heaven, so judging someone based on their flesh pattern is not only damaging, but incredibly deceiving.

God loves you because He loves His Son. He loves you for *who* you are, not what you've done. I relate it to parents who love their children unconditionally, not because of anything they've done or didn't do, but because they belong to them. The amazing truth—far better than the popular belief that we're merely saved sinners—is that we're perfect in God's eyes because we belong to Him. God will never love us any more than He already does! There's no need to try to gain favor or make Him love us more. Scripture tells us in 1 Corinthians 3:16-17 that we are holy because the Spirit of God lives within us. If more Christians took that passage to heart, the Barna research would be much different. If we have Christ dwelling in us, how much more perfect and how much more holy can we possibly be? My prayers often sound like this: "Dear Lord, I don't know what havoc my flesh will cause today, but thank You, Jesus, that I'm perfect in Your eyes!"

I'll end with a quote I ran across in the hallway of Erskine College, where my son attends. It was tacked up unceremoniously on a professor's door on a plain piece of paper, but it might be one of the most important messages of all time outside of Scripture itself. It quotes words of Martin Luther from the year 1516. It reads, "You will never find true peace until you find it and keep it in this…that Christ takes all your sins upon Himself, and bestows all His righteousness upon you." Amen to that.

GOD IS NOT A MICROMANAGER • EVERYONE HAS THEIR OWN FREE WILL • THERE AR
ROADS TO HEAVEN • WHEN WE DIE WE BECOME ANGELS • GOD HELPS THOSE WHO HEL
SELVES • GOD WANTS YOU TO BE RICH • CHRISTIANS AREN'T PERFECT, JUST FORGIVEN
RE GOD'S CO-PILOTS • PRAY HARD AND GOD WILL ANSWER • GOD AND SATAN ARE BATTLIN
T • GOD IS NOT A MICROMANAGER • EVERYONE HAS THEIR OWN FREE WILL • THERE AR
ROADS TO HEAVEN • WHEN WE DIE WE BECOME ANGELS • GOD HELPS THOSE WHO HEL
SELVES • GOD WANTS YOU TO BE RICH • CHRISTIANS AREN'T PERFECT, JUST FORGIVEN
RE GOD'S CO-PILOTS • PRAY HARD AND GOD WILL ANSWER • GOD AND SATAN ARE BATTLIN

CHAPTER 7

BELIEF #6

We Are God's Co-Pilots

H ere's another popular belief I copied down from a bumper sticker while driving one day. I've seen a few variations on this belief. I've seen it phrased in a way that implies God is the captain and we are His helpers, and I've seen it worded to imply that we are the captain and God is there to assist.

I'm not sure which way is scarier. Both suggest, in varying degrees, that God needs us to fulfill His plans. Both suggest a teamlike partnership between us and God. Both suggest that God depends on us to do certain things so He can do His thing—in essence, He can't do it alone. Both are troubling, and most importantly, both are biblically inaccurate.

It seems that this popular belief could be the foundation for several other myths. For example, if you believe the notion that God is your co-pilot, it makes perfect sense that you would think that God will help you more if you help yourself. After all, if it's a true collaboration, both sides might be more willing to help if the other is pulling their weight.

Not Needed, But Wanted

I can't tell you where this belief originated (although I have an idea), but I can tell you that it's firmly planted in pop culture. Just yesterday while I was driving down the road listening to my customary

country music station, a song came on titled "Me and God." I don't
know who the singer was, but some of the lyrics caught my attention.
The very first line of the song was, "There ain't nothing" that God
and I can't do, and the refrain boasted, "We're a team, me and God,"
several times! Now before anyone cries foul, I applaud the writer for so
boldly using God in the song and I recognize the intent was probably
not to make it theologically accurate. But it will no doubt reinforce
the idea that God needs us to complete the team.

The truth is, God doesn't need us at all. God uses us, but He
doesn't need us, nor is He passively waiting for us to do anything.
If God needed us, then He would not be completely sovereign. The
dictionary defines *sovereignty* as "total independence." It doesn't say
partial, limited, or occasional independence. It says *total* independence.

One of the best passages in Scripture to look at is found in Acts
17:24-25:

> God, who made the world and everything in it, since He is
> Lord of heaven and earth, does not dwell in temples made
> with hands. Nor is He worshipped with men's hands, as
> though He needed anything, since He gives to all life, breath,
> and all things.

These simple yet profound verses show us clearly that God doesn't
need us. The key word is *need.* He uses us. He engages and involves
us, but He doesn't *need* us. To believe that God needs us is a very
scary proposition. Never mind that it makes man sovereign because
it puts God in a situation where He might be waiting passively for
us to do something—the thought itself is downright troubling. (I'll
explore that a bit later.)

First, I'd like to explore just how and why we're so attached to the
notion that God needs us. It all goes back to the Garden of Eden. If
you haven't read the story of what happened in the Garden, I highly
recommend it. The story of what happened to Adam and Eve explains

much about the shortcomings and limitations of man. The story can be found in the first book of the Bible, Genesis, in chapters 1, 2, and 3. Allow me to recap the story. In the beginning, God created the heavens and the earth. (I acknowledge that isn't much of a recap since it is taken from Scripture verbatim, but it's tough when you're tinkering with perfection.) God created everything that is in the heavens and the earth. This is supported by many other verses throughout the Bible, notably Colossians 1:16:

> By Him all things were created that are in heaven and that are on earth, visible and invisible, whether thrones or dominions or principalities or powers. All things were created through Him and for Him.

I could stop my argument right there because after all, no created thing is ever needed by its creator, but I'll continue the story. God created man in His image, which is spirit. He created both male and female and gave them run of the Garden. It was a heck of a deal. Adam and Eve lived in Paradise, with a capital P. This was not a virtual paradise, it was the real deal. Right smack in the middle of the Garden, God put the Tree of Life. The Tree of Life was the pathway to heaven. We know this from reading Revelation 22. Think of it. Heaven was once on earth and someday it will be again!

Also in the middle of the Garden was the Tree of the Knowledge of Good and Evil. Contrary to what some may think, this tree was not an evil tree, nor was it a good tree. It was just a tree that held the knowledge of good and evil. God told Adam and Eve that they could and should enjoy Paradise. The only caveat was not to eat any fruit from the Tree of the Knowledge of Good and Evil. God told them that if they ate from that tree, they would surely die.

Well, wouldn't you know it, guess who shows up one night for dinner? Satan. He came as a serpent slithering on the ground around the Tree of the Knowledge of Good and Evil. Now, did you ever wonder where Satan came from? I mean, this was Paradise. This was

God's perfect creation. Did he show up unexpectedly to crash the party? I say absolutely not. More on that in an upcoming chapter, but suffice to say that since God created everything, including Satan,[1] He certainly knew what was going on. God did not turn His back on the Garden for one minute and then look back in surprise. God didn't say to Himself, "Darn that Satan. I was hoping he wouldn't show up!" Satan was there just as God planned.

The serpent lied to Eve and told her she wouldn't die if she ate the forbidden fruit.[2] The serpent then told her the most damaging lie ever conceived: The reason God didn't want her to eat from that tree was because if she did, she would become like God. The serpent told her that her eyes would be opened and she would become wise.

Well, as you already know, Eve ate the fruit, gave some to Adam, and instantly they knew the difference between good and evil. They instantly became aware they were both naked, and felt ashamed. They also both died at that moment. No, they didn't die physically. They died spiritually. At that moment, they became separated from God, and so it is to this day, until we become born again.

Pride Appeal

There are many relevant truths to gain from this story, and I admittedly am passing over many, but for the purpose of trying to shed light on why man clings so tightly to the notion that God needs us, let's focus on the lie Satan used in the Garden. There's more to the curse of the Garden than spiritual death. That moment falsely elevated the stature of man. Satan played to the most basic, yet most powerful, of all human emotions: vanity.

> Satan has only this one lie and he milks it for all it's worth. All human sins find their roots in vanity.

Adam and Eve wanted to be like God. They didn't want to be Indians. They wanted to be chiefs. They wanted to be more important. They wanted better jobs. They wanted a bigger house. They wanted nicer things. They wanted to be like God, and most of all, they wanted God to need them too. They wanted some of the glory.

So do we. The idea that God needs us, even in the smallest way, is appealing to our human condition. Pride and vanity are an inseparable part of our flesh. We want to be needed. We want glory and, despite our admissions, it's hard to give all the glory to God. Even as I know I am nothing and God is everything, I still delight in being in the limelight. I still crave my just rewards for my hard work. I like my social status and I like it when people buy my books.

I, like you, am trapped inside the flesh, which is still under the curse of the Garden. Satan has only this one lie and he milks it for all it's worth. All human sins find their roots in vanity. This is why Jesus warned repeatedly of the dangers of vanity and preached the importance of humility.

Matthew 18:4 and Matthew 23:12 are great verses to memorize. The latter verse reads, "Whoever exalts himself will be humbled and he who humbles himself will be exalted." Jesus was teaching the importance of not getting too caught up in worldly, vain trappings of the flesh. Paul, who wrote most of the New Testament, also repeatedly warned against vanity. In 1 Corinthians 8:1-2, he wrote,

> Knowledge puffs up, but love edifies. And if anyone thinks
> that he knows anything, he knows nothing yet as he ought
> to know.

It's interesting that Paul used the term *puffed up*. In modern language, we would call it a big head or getting too big for our britches. The natural consequence of getting puffed up is a lesser reliance on God. If you're honest with yourself, you know this to be true on an experiential level. The more worldly success one seems to have, the less dependent on God one is.

I find myself praying more, studying more, and worshipping more when I am most down in the dumps. It's at those times I realize my weaknesses and turn more to God. Conversely, when things are going great and everything seems to happen easily and effortlessly, the human condition kicks in and I find myself less reliant on God. It's for this reason that worldly success is often a detriment to a deeper relationship with the Lord. Of course, it doesn't need to be this way, nor should it be, but it often happens. Worldly success and riches bring out the vanity. It's almost as if the serpent is right there with us saying those words all over again: "You can be like God."

What helps me are the words of Paul in 2 Corinthians 12:5-6:

> Of myself I will not boast, except in my infirmities. For though I might desire to boast, I will not be a fool; for I will speak the truth.

Paul wrote several times that the only thing we should boast in is when we are weak. It's when we are weak that we are most strong because of our dependence on God.[3]

I also get a daily reminder of the only thing that is worthy of actual boasting. The words of Galatians 6:14 are etched on a hanging cross and displayed prominently on my bedroom wall. They read, *But God forbid that I should boast except in the cross of our Lord Jesus Christ, by whom the world has been crucified to me, and I to the world.* This passage sums up everything I've spent the past few pages writing about. If we're a new creation in Christ (as we've learned in the previous chapter), then we are no longer of this world. Through the blood shed by Christ, we have been crucified to the things of this world. It profits us nothing to brag about worldly things because they are only temporary and are of much less value than the riches that await us in heaven. The only boasting we should ever do is that we belong to Christ. This is precisely what Adam and Eve should have said to Satan. They should have said, "I've got all I need." But instead they got caught up in the beauty of the fruit and the idea of more power. It's the curse of the flesh, and we have Adam and Eve to thank for it.

God's "Main Man"?

So God doesn't need us despite the fact that we like to think He does. But consider for a moment if this popular belief were true. What if God did need us? What if God couldn't do the things He intended to do without our help?

Well, first off, as I mentioned previously, I would argue that if God couldn't do the things He intended to do without our help, then God would not be completely sovereign. Picture this for a moment: God watching anxiously from heaven hoping we would make the choice He intended for us and then slapping His knee, saying "Good grief, I was hoping Sally would do something else." That is certainly not a vision of a sovereign God. But if that was the case, just imagine how scary things would be. I'll cover this again in the chapter "God Is Not a Micromanager," but suffice it to say that if God really did need us, we could never find true peace and rest. If the fate of our outcome, let alone the world, lay in what we did as God passively looked on from above, how could anyone find peace?

Are you thinking I'm taking it to the extreme? Maybe you respond that God is neither totally passive nor is He a control freak. He merely allows us to take control of the cockpit at times, but is right there to guide us and help us. He is our co-pilot. But it's still the same argument. If God truly allows us to take control of the cockpit, it stands to reason we might fly left when He wanted us to fly right. We might lose altitude when He wanted us to gain altitude.

Either way, if we could do something different from that which God would have us do, then God is not completely in control. He would not be completely sovereign. After all, co-pilots need the pilot, and the pilot needs the co-pilot. One needs the other. That isn't the way it is with God. We need God, but God doesn't need us. The idea that we are anything "co" with God is a false one. Again, God loves us and uses us to accomplish His will, but let's not get a big head. God is God. We'll never be like God, despite what the serpent might want us to believe. He doesn't need us.

Booted Off the Team

What we need is a nice dose of humility. This is precisely what Jesus had in mind in Matthew 18:1-4:

> At that time the disciples came to Jesus, saying "Who then is greatest in the kingdom of heaven?" Then Jesus called a little child to Him, set him in the midst of them, and said, "Assuredly, I say to you, unless you are converted and become as little children, you will by no means enter the kingdom of heaven. Therefore whoever humbles himself as this little child is the greatest in the kingdom of heaven."

A couple of things jump out at me in that passage. First, Jesus talked of the process of becoming childlike as a conversion. I believe He was talking about being born again. Children of the flesh are not necessarily children that will enter the kingdom of heaven. Children of the flesh inherited the position from Adam and Eve and think like the world. Children of heaven are born again. They are converted back to their original state (the one originally given to Adam and Eve) of total dependence on God.

The second thing that jumps out to me is that Jesus calls us to be humble. Children totally need another person. A young child cannot be self-sufficient. A child is not sovereign. A child is not totally independent. A child cannot be someone's co-pilot. A child is helpless. That is a humbling position. That is the position Jesus was teaching. Charles Spurgeon, the great writer and preacher of the nineteenth century, once said, "Humility is to make the right estimate of yourself." I love that quote. I often don't make the right estimate of myself, but the right estimate is one that is totally dependent on God.

The truth is, we're not only not co-pilots, we're not even in the cockpit at all. We're back in coach. God is the pilot, the co-pilot, the engineer, the inventor, the machinist, the fuel, and anything else that is needed to fly the plane. That's why God is God—and believe it or not, God likes being God!

I can't speak for all believers, but I wouldn't want it any other way. If left to us, in any capacity, the world is in trouble. If there was even one single believer out there who really was God's co-pilot, they might choose to zig when God wanted to zag. The world would be even scarier than it is, and no one could find peace and rest, but thankfully He's solidly and solely at the helm. We can rest in Him. Again, another quote from Martin Luther hits the nail on the head. (Can you tell I admire Luther's teachings?) "God created the world out of nothing, and as long as we are nothing, He can make something out of us." Let's glory in being nothing!

GOD IS NOT A MICROMANAGER • EVERYONE HAS THEIR OWN FREE WILL • THERE AR
ROADS TO HEAVEN • WHEN WE DIE WE BECOME ANGELS • GOD HELPS THOSE WHO HEL
SELVES • GOD WANTS YOU TO BE RICH • CHRISTIANS AREN'T PERFECT, JUST FORGIVEN
RE GOD'S CO-PILOTS • PRAY HARD AND GOD WILL ANSWER • GOD AND SATAN ARE BATTLIN
T • GOD IS NOT A MICROMANAGER • EVERYONE HAS THEIR OWN FREE WILL • THERE AR
ROADS TO HEAVEN • WHEN WE D   NGELS • GOD HELPS THOSE WHO HEL
SELVES • GOD WANTS YOU TO BE RICH • CHRISTIANS AREN'T PERFECT, JUST FORGIVEN
                              PRAY HARD AND GOD WILL ANSWER •

CHAPTER 8

BELIEF #7

Pray Hard and God Will Answer

The Bible is loaded with instances when God answered prayers, like in 1 Samuel 1:27, when Samuel prayed and the Lord answered. Indeed the Lord answered, but the question is, Did the Lord grant Samuel's request because he made an eloquent case, or did the Lord use Samuel's prayer as a means to do what He had always intended to do? I contend the latter.

Probably nothing is as misunderstood in the Christian world as prayer. Prayer has become the spiritual text message of the twenty-first century. All you need to do is make your request to God, follow it up with fervent petitioning, and your prayers can be answered. This idea that prayers can affect God's plan is a direct extension of the previous popular belief that we are God's co-pilots. As with the co-pilot myth, the belief that prayers can change God's mind is a direct result of believing we're more important than we really are. The image of God listening intently to our feeble arguments as to why our prayers should be granted and deciding to grant them or not based on the logic, duration, frequency, or passionateness of our request is one that I find very hard to comprehend.

Nonetheless, as absurd as it may sound, many churches seem to teach this very concept. I've quoted one pastor of a prominent national church as saying, "If you can rally enough faith and truly believe that your prayers will be answered, God cannot turn away!" I've heard yet another say, "The more people you have praying for your petition, the louder God hears you." Let's look at each one of those statements a bit closer because both are not only biblically incorrect, they are tremendously damaging as well.

You Supply the Faith, God Supplies Your Wants

Both statements at their core suggest that we control the destiny of our own prayers—that we can determine the outcome. Here I again beat the same drum of sovereignty—if that was the case, God would not be sovereign. *We* would be, or at very least, *prayer* would be. The first statement suggests we can get our prayers answered by mustering up enough faith. This is taught by the "Prosperity Gospel" proponents. All you have to do is name and claim it. But how much faith is enough faith? Does this mean that the times when God seemingly answered your prayers, you had enough faith, and the times He didn't, it was because your faith was lacking? The long and short answer is *no*. Prayer is not God's litmus test to determine the level of your faith.

> If it were possible to dictate the outcome of a prayer, it would certainly give someone a really good reason to boast.

This hit home personally with me several years ago when my second child and eldest boy was going through a battery of tests on his liver and bile ducts. The doctors were baffled and to say the least, it was a very stressful time in the Rich household. One of our closest friends offered their thoughts on the matter. They told us that if we prayed hard enough, we could heal our son's affliction. They meant well, but after thinking about their comment for a minute or two, I realized it was quite cruel. Thankfully, I immediately chalked it up to another misguided believer who had accepted a popular belief as doctrine.

It actually was a major impetus in wanting to write this book, but what if I had believed my friend's advice? What if the fate of my son really did lie in my hands? I know they were trying to empower me.

I know they wanted me to believe God would cure him, but that is a monster of a burden to place on a person's shoulders. I never doubted God *could* cure my son; the only question was whether God *would* cure him. If I falsely believed it was up to my faith, how is that fair to my son? Would he be held accountable for my lack of enough faith? Prayer would become a burden and a chore instead of the awesome means of experiencing grace it is now.

And think of this—if it were possible to dictate the outcome of a prayer, it would certainly give someone a really good reason to boast. *Nanny, nanny, boo-boo, my prayer was answered, I've got more faith than you!* Imagine the books and the claims certain preachers might make. I can hear someone saying right now they've discovered the secret to getting prayers answered. Someone might lay claim to having an inside track.

This, of course, is contrary to Scripture. The book of Daniel, chapter 4, verse 35, is one of the best passages to defend the sovereignty of God. It says,

> All the inhabitants of the earth are reputed as nothing; He does according to His will in the army of heaven *and* among the inhabitants of the earth. No one can restrain His hand or say to Him, What have you done?

That passage is pretty specific. No one can say to God, "Why did you do that?" or "Why didn't you do that?" God does what God decides is best and we inhabitants of the earth don't amount to much in that category.

The Bible also maintains in Ephesians 1:11 that God works all things according to the counsel of His will. That passage says *all things,* not just some things. Not just the ones you'll bring to Him somewhere down the line in prayer, but all things, known or unknown. The passage also says that God does according to His will. God knows what is best and He knows how all the pieces fit together for His glory. Romans 8:28 uses the phrase again, *"All things* work together for good to those who love God." We only know the micro spec of information as it pertains to us. We don't know the big picture. Fortunately, God does and it is His sovereign will that prevails.

A Question of Quantity

The second statement I want to dissect concerns intercessory prayer. Too many Christians have a misunderstanding about intercessory prayer. Too many believe it's a question of quantity. I can't tell you how many Christians believe that the more people they can solicit to pray for something, the better their odds at getting their prayers answered.

Intercessory prayer is a good thing, and quite frankly, it is a pro-actively caring thing to do for someone in need, but there's no magic number to hit that all of a sudden perks up God's ears. If the key to prayer were as simple as having a certain number of people praying, it would wipe out the need for faith. Where there's a formula, faith is irrelevant.

If indeed there were a magic formula to getting prayers answered, we could never rest. Prayer would become an absolute burden instead of the wonderful fellowship it was intended to be. If you knew that all you had to do was solicit as many people as you could on your behalf and your prayer would be answered, you would never cease in the quest to sign up more people. Eventually everyone would be praying for everyone and prayer would no longer be pleasurable. It would be a chore. You'd be doing it out of obligation and for selfish motives.

Not to mention that prayer would then be sovereign over God. If an act can dictate an outcome, then the act is more powerful than the person. Thankfully, that is not the way it is. God alone is sovereign and prayer is a means God uses to accomplish His will, but it cannot change His plans. Regardless of the number of people praying, the way we pray, which direction we face, or how much belief we have that God will answer our prayers, God has a plan and we cannot alter it.

I can't speak for you, but this gives me great peace. It's not up to me. The fate of my child, much less the fate of the world, does not lie in the mechanics of prayer. I can trust that God knows best and that whatever happens is what He ordained. I may not understand it. I may not like it. I may not agree with it, but everything happens for His glory. He knows how everything fits together. He knows the beginnings and the ends and all things in between. God is an awesome God and we just need to trust that we will never even come close to knowing what God knows.

When we are facing a major surgery, we trust the wisdom, knowledge, and experience of a trained surgeon. When we fly in an airplane, we trust blindly in the capabilities of a captain we may never see. When we eat at a restaurant, we trust that the food we eat was prepared properly by someone who knows what they are doing. All those examples are of mere people with many flaws, and sometimes things do go wrong. Yet, we trust every day. Why not trust God blindly? God has no flaws. God makes no mistakes and since He makes no mistakes, we can trust that what happens must have happened for a reason. King Solomon, who many historians hail as one of the wisest men who has ever lived, wrote this in Proverbs 3:5: "Trust in the LORD with all your heart and lean not on your own understanding." Trust God—"for of Him and through Him and to Him are *all things* to whom be glory forever. Amen."[1]

Why Pray?

So, you might be asking, what exactly is the role of prayer? If God's gonna do what God's gonna do, why pray at all? If I had a dollar for every time someone said that to me in rebuttal, I'd have long retired by now. The answer is a simple one. We pray because we want to. We pray because we are led by the Spirit to do so. We pray because we are new creations in Christ and His Spirit lives in us. It is that indwelling Spirit that leads us to pray. Sure, we often end up praying humanly for things that may or may not be in God's plan, but through prayer we are connected to God and are part of what He is doing in our lives. The Spirit intercedes on our behalf and aligns our requests with God's will, as Romans 8:26 tells us:

> The Spirit also helps in our weaknesses. For we do not know what we should pray for as we ought, but the Spirit Himself makes intercession for us with groanings which cannot be uttered. Now He who searches the hearts knows what the mind of the Spirit is, because He makes intercession for the saints according to the will of God.

We do not know what we should pray for nor are we even qualified to know because we are still in our human shell. However, the Spirit inside knows and is constantly in communication with the Father.

Paul wrote further about the role of the Spirit in prayer in 1 Corinthians 2:11: "What man knows the things of a man except the spirit of the man which is in him? Even so no one knows the things of God except the Spirit of God." Our job is simply to pray when led to pray and then trust the outcome. James tells us how we should pray in James 4:15. In verse 13 he is writing about our inability to know the future and that sets up verse 15, where he tells us that we should say, "If the Lord wills, we shall live and do this or that."

This is precisely the way Jesus prayed and how He taught His disciples how to pray. You might recall the prayer Jesus prayed in the Garden of Gethsemane. The prayer is told in several of the Gospels, but I'll reference Luke 22:41-42:

> He was withdrawn from them about a stone's throw, and He knelt down and prayed, saying, "Father, if it is Your will, take this cup away from Me; nevertheless not My will, but Yours be done."

Jesus was in human form, so He couldn't help but ask God to rescue Him from what He knew was about to take place, but He also knew that He wasn't about to alter the Father's plans. So, I ask you, if Jesus knew that He couldn't alter God's plans through prayer, what makes us think we can?

Jesus also taught His disciples how to pray in Luke 11:2-4. This is known as "The Lord's Prayer." It is without doubt the most common prayer spoken. I want to draw particular attention to the words "Your kingdom come, Your will be done on earth as it is heaven." Jesus is teaching His disciples that it isn't our will that will be done, but rather God's will that will be done.

It is in that light that we should also pray. There is nothing wrong with bringing our requests to God through prayer, or even pleading our case with God, but we should end every prayer with "but not my will but Your will be done." Trusting and accepting the outcome of our prayers is the basis behind the passage in Philippians 4:6: "Be anxious for nothing, but in everything by prayer and supplication, with thanksgiving, let your requests be made known to God." Plead your case, but do it with thanksgiving, knowing the outcome will be exactly what God has planned for you.

Freedom Through Trust

One of my all-time favorite biblical stories is the story of Shadrach, Meshach, and Abed-Nego, as told in Daniel 3:8-18. (I briefly made reference to this story in chapter 2.) You recall King Nebuchadnezzar commanded them to worship the gold image he had set up. The king told them that if they did not comply, they would be thrown into a burning, fiery furnace. Shadrach, Meshach, and Abed-Nego were brought before the king. Verses 16 through 18 give their reply:

> O Nebuchadnezzar, we have no need to answer you in this matter. If that is the case, our God whom we serve is able to deliver us from the burning fiery furnace and He will deliver us from your hand, O king. But if not, let it be known to you, O king, that we do not serve your gods, nor will we worship the gold image which you have set up.

They were, of course, cast into the furnace, and they were delivered just as they had hoped. They were rescued as on wings of eagles as I have written about previously.

The part I want to focus on here is their response before they were cast into the furnace. They prayed that God would deliver them, but they also said three of the most liberating words of the entire Bible, "but if not." They made their requests known to God through prayer and supplication, but they understood that it wasn't their will but rather God's will that was going to happen, and they were at peace with that. They said that they believed God would rescue them, *but if not,* they were okay with it because their God was still God. They trusted the outcome, no matter what was in store.

This is how we should pray. Pray as you're led to pray. Pray hard and plead your case with supplication and passion, but in the end, say, "but if not," and give glory and thanksgiving to God. This is what brings true peace. *Peace is not gained through always getting the answer from God that you wanted, but instead, it is gained through trusting and accepting whatever answer you get.*

I love the song by Martina McBride called "Anyway." It's one of the most inspiring songs I've ever heard, and it makes an incredibly powerful statement about prayer. Even though God is great, as she says, sometimes life isn't good. It doesn't always come out the way we think it ought to. But then, she affirms, she does it "anyway." That's the biblical truth about prayer in a nutshell. Though things don't always turn out like we want them to turn out, we continue to pray nonetheless.

> Our hope completely begins and ends with God. He alone is in charge and knows how everything fits together.

We pray because we are absolutely driven to pray. We pray because we recognize our need for a Savior. We need help. We pray because we know it's the most powerful thing we can do. Not because it will change God's plan, but because our hope completely begins and ends with God. He alone is in charge and knows how everything fits together. We also pray because we're thankful. Prayer is God's ordained means to help us feel connected with His plan. We sometimes fall to our knees in humble prayer, thankful that He knows better than us. Sometimes I've been known to thank God profusely for not answering a few of my prayers. His plan for my life turned out to be much better than what I thought should happen. Thankfully, His Spirit intervened.

A final test to gauge your prayer life is this: Prayer should always lead to peace and assurance that God is in charge. If prayer is a burden and you do it out of a sense of obligation, you will not find peace. If prayer leads to becoming more uneasy, then you're not trusting God. You're trying to affect God. The bottom line is you're either trying or trusting. Trying leads to unrest, trusting leads to peace.

My prayer is that this book will help you find greater peace and rest through biblical truth instead of popular belief, but if not, God has you right where He wants you. He alone is sovereign and He will do what He wants to do. Prayer will help you feel connected to what God has planned, but there isn't a magic prayer formula that can change His mind. He is great. When life isn't good, and your prayers don't come out like you think they should, the good news is, you can always trust God. He knows what you need and how everything fits together in His plan. Pray as you're led, and leave the outcome to God.

• GOD IS NOT A MICROMANAGER • EVERYONE HAS THEIR OWN FREE WILL • THERE AR
ROADS TO HEAVEN • WHEN WE DIE WE BECOME ANGELS • GOD HELPS THOSE WHO HEL
SELVES • GOD WANTS YOU TO BE RICH • CHRISTIANS AREN'T PERFECT, JUST FORGIVEN
RE GOD'S CO-PILOTS • PRAY HARD AND GOD WILL ANSWER • GOD AND SATAN ARE BATTLIN
T • GOD IS NOT A MICROMANAGER • EVERYONE HAS THEIR OWN FREE WILL • THERE AR
ROADS TO HEAVEN • WHEN WE DIE WE BECOME ANGELS • GOD HELPS THOSE WHO HEL
SELVES • GOD WANTS YOU TO BE RICH • CHRISTIANS AREN'T PERFECT, JUST FORGIVEN
RE GOD'S CO-PILOTS • PRAY HARD AND GOD WILL ANSWER • GOD AND SATAN ARE BATTLIN

CHAPTER 9

BELIEF #8

God and Satan Are Battling It Out

If I hear one more sermon on the battle between good and evil, I might cause a scene. You know how at a wedding the minister asks if anyone has an objection to the marriage let them speak up or forever hold their peace? Well, I might just speak up next time I hear a preacher exhorting us in regard to the cosmic battle between God and Satan.

I'm sure you know exactly the kind of sermon I am referring to. One that warns us that Satan is winning the war and we'd better step up our Christianly efforts, or one that reports that the earth is going to hell in a handbasket, just look at all the natural disasters for proof, or one that blasts us with the news that the attack on 9/11 was because Satan is running amuck.

And that's just half of the battle. One half may be the battle as we see it play out in the world around us; the other half is the battle for our souls. The following is a few lines from a sermon I watched on TV not too long ago: "Once you submit to God and become a Christian, then the real war begins. Satan will relentlessly attack you in his effort to win you back. Satan does not like being defeated and he will wage battle with you until the very end. So, my friends, hold on tight. If you loosen your grip even the slightest, Satan will reclaim you!" This blows my mind. It is no wonder that many Christians have become disillusioned with religion and are living more in fear than they are in peace. It's one thing to see evil around us and perhaps believe God is losing the battle, but to even think for one moment that your very salvation could be up for grabs is far more scary!

The good news is, neither is true. Satan is not winning the battle of the world, and he certainly is not, and will not, win the battle for your soul. Satan has already lost both fronts. I wanted to clear that up right up front in this chapter. Satan wants you to believe he is winning, but it is nothing more than a lie. I'll explore more on the truth in a bit, but first look at why we believe the lie in the first place.

Some Perspective Is Needed

The obvious answer is we see it with our own eyes. Evil is all around us. All you need to do is turn on the nightly news and it's easy to become depressed. I was a journalism major in college and among journalists there is a saying that is sadistic, but sadly true. The saying is, "If it bleeds, it leads." That means that if there is blood and gore in the story, it becomes the lead story. Violence gets you to the head of the pack. As sick as that sounds, it's a chicken-or-the-egg question. News broadcasts put those stories on because that's what catches our eyes. News shows, like any other show, only care about ratings. If we didn't watch, they would change their ways. They don't because we tune in.

I have several theories about this, but the main one is that it's because we can identify with evil. We can see evil. We can't see God. In fact, in every poll, no one doubts the existence of evil. Not everyone may believe in a devil per se, but everyone believes evil is rampant. Contrast that with the polls about God. In a Harris Poll conducted between October 4 and 10, 2006, with a sample of over 2000 U.S. adults, 42 percent reported that they are not "absolutely certain" there is a God, including 15 percent who said they were only "somewhat certain." Add to that the 11 percent who said they think there is probably no God, and 16 percent who said they weren't sure and you come up with only 31 percent who said they believed without a doubt there was a God. That's not even defining the God of the Bible. Many believe in a god, but not God. Check out the shelves of any bookstore and you'll see that. Books about a god are plentiful, but books about the God of Scripture lag behind.

Clearly, we know evil. When we see a child get abducted and killed, many cry out, "How can there be a God?" It's a fair question, but are we capable of judging? The Bible says our judgment is impaired by human eyes. We don't see the big picture. It reminds me of stories I've read about Normandy in World War II. In almost every interview with surviving ground troops, they all said the same thing. They said they were certain they would be defeated. From their perspective, they were outnumbered and outflanked. However, in interviews with fighter pilots that flew above the action, they all said they knew we would be victorious. From their perspective, it was clear we had the upper hand from the very beginning of the invasion.

The difference of course is view. One was limited, while the other had the benefit of seeing what the other couldn't. Same with God. We don't see how, nor can we imagine how an evil act could possibly fit into God's bigger plan, but our view is limited. Our view is tainted with human eyes. What's evil by worldly standards may not be to God.

Take a look at Genesis 50:20: "As for you, you meant evil against me; but God meant it for good, in order to bring it about as it is to this day, to save many people alive." The world may see something as evil, but God means it for a greater good. The attack of 9/11 is but one of countless examples. The stories of all the wonderful good that came out of that tragedy continue to humble and amaze me. I am still saddened for the families of the victims, but I hope they can find some peace in knowing that thousands, if not millions, of people were led to God as a result of that act.

The Bible also says, in Psalm 116:15, "Precious in the sight of the LORD is the death of His saints." That's right. It isn't misquoted. God rejoices when one of His saints joins Him in Paradise. Because of our limited perspective, we have things backward. We celebrate old age as if it was some kind of reward for good living and mourn when a baby dies. What if, in heaven, it was the other way around? What if in heaven the saints all say, "God, why are you letting that 80-year-old continue to live?" and "Praise be to God that He brought this little one home so soon!" It's all a matter of perspective.

As for the battle of our own souls, the answer is the same. We have an earthly perspective. We see sin every day in ourselves and that causes us to doubt our own salvation. That's why it is imperative that we understand who we are. We are not our flesh. Our own arms and legs are aliens to our real identity. If necessary, reread chapter 6.

Evil may be around us and still in our fleshly bodies, but that doesn't mean that evil is winning or that it ever will win. It's easy to believe evil is winning because that's what we see with our limited scope and human eyes, but we must have faith in what God sees. I love the Bible's definition of faith. It's found in Hebrews 11:1, "Now faith is the substance of things hoped for, the evidence of things not seen." We need to have faith that God is in charge and always at work, even if we don't see it or recognize it as such.

Satan—Not to Worry!

So what's the big deal? Why is not having faith or believing that Satan is winning the battle so harmful to believe? The answer is all about peace. Have you ever had a time when you felt completely scared about something only to find out later that you had absolutely nothing to be frightened about? You wished that you had known then what you know now.

That's precisely the answer to our question. You wouldn't fear Satan near as much if you knew that God was in charge and that Satan doesn't operate outside God's bounds. You wouldn't fear Satan near as much if you knew that once you became a born-again new creature belonging to Jesus that Satan cannot ever cause you to lose your way. Well, praise God, both are true! Let's look at both battles—the one in the world and the one over our personal salvation. I hope you too will conclude that you have nothing to fear from Satan.

The Bible is very clear. Satan does not and cannot operate outside of God's authority. I gave you lots of biblical passages in the last chapter that used the phrase "all things." Remember Colossians 1:16 says that all things, both visible and invisible, were created by Him, through Him, and for Him. The creator always has sovereignty over the creation. Satan does not do anything outside of God's dominion.

I know that may seem like a tough truth to swallow, but consider the alternative. To believe Satan can do anything outside of God's providence means that God is not completely sovereign. It would mean that the passages in Scripture that say "all things" don't include Satan. It would mean that even though the Bible ultimately speaks of Satan's demise, that may or may not be true. If God and Satan are on equal footing, the Bible may just be God's version of events. Satan may have his own version of events.

> God may place us in some scary places, but that isn't by accident. It is all by design.

Thankfully, even Satan knows deep down that God is in complete control. Nothing catches God off guard. Things that appear to be evil are still all part of God's plan. My favorite passage to illustrate this is found in three of the Gospels—Matthew, Mark, and Luke. In Matthew 4, Mark 1, and Luke 4, you will notice that Jesus was led into the wilderness to be tempted by Satan. Who was doing the leading? In all three accounts, Jesus was led by the Holy Spirit. Mark's account describes it this way:

> The *Spirit* drove Him into the wilderness. And He was there forty days, tempted by Satan, and was with the wild beasts; and the angels ministered to Him (1:12-13).

Note it wasn't Satan who did the driving. It wasn't even Jesus' own will that led Him. Jesus was led by God. If Jesus was to fear anything or anybody, it shouldn't be Satan. It should be God.

Therein lies a powerful truth. We shouldn't fear Satan. We should trust God. God may place us in some scary places, but that isn't by accident. It is all by design.

"Yea, though I walk through the valley of the shadow of death, I fear no evil; for You are with me." That's perhaps one of the most commonly recited passages of the Bible. It's from Psalm 23:4. Another of the most commonly recited passages is the Lord's Prayer, found in Matthew 6. One line is particularly relevant to this discussion. It's found in Matthew 6:13, "Do not lead us into temptation, but deliver us from the evil one." Notice again who Jesus speaks of as doing the leading. It is God. God is in charge of all things, and Satan is not going to wreck God's plans.

Satan's Bounds Are Limited

On the personal salvation front, I'll go one step further. I believe Satan cannot do one single harmful thing to a believer unless God specifically grants him permission. There are two prominent examples of this truth in Scripture. The first is found in the story of Job. I will certainly paraphrase part of the story but I highly recommend reading it from beginning to end. It's one of the most inspiring and truth-filled books of the Bible.

Job was a good man. He was a pillar of the community and had seven sons and three daughters. God Himself even called Job "a blameless and upright man, one who fears God and shuns evil."[1] One day, seemingly out of the blue, God offered up Job to Satan. This is an important truth to grasp because we see in Scripture that Satan did not bring up Job's name. It was God. God said, "Have you considered My servant Job?" (1:8). Satan, naturally, was skeptical. In verse 10 Satan replied, "Have you not made a hedge around him, around his household, and around all that he has on every side?" Satan knew that Job belonged to God. In fact, *all* believers have a hedge around them that Satan cannot penetrate.

But God had a plan for Job that included some heartache and misery. God gave permission to Satan to torment Job and make his life miserable, but added very clearly in verse 12 of chapter 1, "Only do not lay a hand on his person." This meant that Satan could torment and disrupt his life, but that Satan was not to harm him physically. It is interesting to note that Satan operated exactly within the bounds set by God. Satan did indeed torment Job. Satan caused a great wind to blow that destroyed his property and killed his children, but Job continued to bless the name of the Lord.

Once again, God initiated a dialogue with Satan and for a second time, offered up Job to Satan. Satan replied, "Skin for skin! Yes, all that a man has he will give for his life. But stretch out Your hand now and touch his bone and his flesh, and he will surely curse You to Your face!" (2:4-5). So, once again, God granted Satan permission to torment Job, but again added that Satan was not to kill him. Once again, Satan operated within the bounds set by God. Job immediately was struck with extremely painful boils over his entire body. In fact, things got a whole lot worse for Job before they got better.

God eventually fully restored Job, and Scripture tells us that Job's latter days were more blessed than his beginning, but let's focus on Satan for a moment. One would think that if Satan was indeed God's nemesis, Satan would not listen to God's commands. Satan might go along with God when he was with Him, but then do as he pleased. I would think that if there was really a battle between God and Satan, Satan would seize every opportunity to win the battle. I would think that if Satan was out to defeat God's plan, he would have harmed Job physically the first time and would have killed him the second time. He surely would not have listened to God.

But that's precisely what he did. Satan did not disobey God because he *could not* disobey God. God alone is sovereign, and that includes being sovereign over the forces of evil. Job's own prayer to God in Job 14:1,5 reminds us of this truth:

> Man who is born of woman is of few days and full of trouble...
> Since his days are determined, the number of his months is with
> You; You have appointed his limits, so that he cannot pass.

In 42:2, Job also acknowledges, "No purpose of Yours can be withheld from You." Job recognized he had nothing to fear from Satan because God was in charge of everything, and whatever happened did so because that's what God had planned. Job didn't fear Satan. He feared how he might be used by God.

The other prominent example is in the Gospels and occurs at the Last Supper. In the Gospel of Luke 22:31, Jesus tells Peter that Satan had asked God for permission to torment him, to "sift you as wheat," were the exact words. Jesus told Peter that He intervened and prayed that Peter's faith would not fail, but God must have granted Satan limited permission, as He did with Job, because Peter went out and denied Jesus three times, but ultimately never lost his faith.

☐ ☐ ☐

I believe these examples are a picture of the way it is with all believers. We belong to God and Satan cannot do anything to us unless granted permission by God, and he certainly cannot rob us of our salvation. In John 10:28, when Jesus is speaking of His sheep (believers), He says most plainly, "I give them eternal life, and they shall never perish; neither shall anyone snatch them out of My hand." It's so important that Jesus repeats His words again in the next verse: "My Father who has given them to Me is greater than all; and no one is able to snatch them out of My Father's hand. I and My Father are one." Jesus didn't say "No one except maybe Satan." Jesus said that God is greater than *all* and that *no one* can snatch a believer out of His hand.

This is also what is meant in Ephesians 1:13-14 when Paul wrote,

> In Him you also trusted, after you heard the word of truth, the gospel of your salvation; in whom also, having believed, you were sealed with the Holy Spirit of promise, who is the guarantee of our inheritance until the redemption of the purchased possession to the praise of His glory.

The purchased possession is you and you are sealed by the Holy Spirit. Satan may get permission to make your life miserable, but he'll never rob you of your salvation. Your inheritance is guaranteed.

An even stronger passage is Romans 8:38-39:

> I am persuaded that neither death nor life, nor angels, nor principalities nor powers, nor things present nor things to come, nor height nor depth, nor any other created thing, shall be able to separate us from the love of God which is in Christ Jesus our Lord.

Paul was pretty thorough. Nothing can separate you from God!

The bottom line: Satan is not running amuck; he is controlled by God, and his end has already been determined. We know he has already been defeated. God's work is finished. The end has been written, but since we still live in a world governed by time, we may experience a few minor battles with Satan, but only those ordained by God. And no battle will rob us of eternal life. Think of it this way, if Satan had even a slight glimmer of hope, then we would have to have a slight glimmer of doubt. Thank God, Satan has no hope, so we should have no doubt! That's a truth you can rest on.

· GOD IS NOT A MICROMANAGER · EVERYONE HAS THEIR OWN FREE WILL · THERE AR
ROADS TO HEAVEN · WHEN WE DIE WE BECOME ANGELS · GOD HELPS THOSE WHO HEL
ELVES · GOD WANTS YOU TO BE RICH · CHRISTIANS AREN'T PERFECT, JUST FORGIVEN ·
E GOD'S CO-PILOTS · PRAY HARD AND GOD WILL ANSWER · GOD AND SATAN ARE BATTLIN(
T · GOD IS NOT A MICROMANAGER · EVERYONE HAS THEIR OWN FREE WILL · THERE AR
ROADS TO HEAVEN · WHEN WE ... ... ANGELS · GOD HELPS THOSE WHO HEL
ELVES · GOD WANTS YOU TO BE RICH · CHRISTIANS AREN'T PERFECT, JUST FORGIVEN ·
E GOD'S CO-PILOTS · PRAY HARD AND GOD WILL ANSWER · ... ...

CHAPTER 10

BELIEF #9

God Is Not a Micromanager

You might not have heard this popular belief stated exactly this way before, but you've probably heard it before in many other ways. The belief is that God is not a micromanager. God isn't, and can't be, in all the minute details.

The implications of misunderstanding God's role are serious. This belief suggests that God sometimes takes a backseat and leaves things up to us. It suggests that our very own salvation is up to us. God is ready and willing when we are, but it's our call. It also suggests that God doesn't want to be intrusive and that He doesn't intervene in the small details of this world. Lastly, it suggests that if Adam and Eve hadn't screwed up, things would be a lot different today. While I can't completely disagree with that statement, I contend that Adam and Eve didn't so much "screw up" as they did exactly what God had planned for them.

This chapter will focus on three things: God's role in the Garden, God's role in your salvation, and God's role in day-to-day life on earth. I believe that God is a micromanager, and I wouldn't want it any other way.

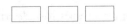

First, let's look at God's role in creation. God was not an indifferent bystander as the world was created. I guess from that statement, you can tell that I'm not a huge believer in evolution. In whatever way creatures and plant life may have developed through the years, it was all by the providential design of a sovereign God. God created all processes, just as He did everything else in the universe. I get that from the first line of the Bible: "In the beginning, God created the heavens and the earth." The entire first chapter of the Bible explains how God created everything, including mankind, and even Lucifer, who was originally a beautiful archangel and then rebelled against God and took an army of angels along with him.

I know there is a specific purpose in everything God does. So, when Satan popped up in the Garden in the form of a serpent, it didn't catch God by surprise. God had a plan from the very beginning. One of the many passages that make this clear is Revelation 13:8 where it is written that the Lamb was "slain before the foundation of the world." The Lamb, of course, is Jesus, and God had a redemptive plan to reclaim His sheep before the episode in the Garden ever took place. Jesus was not a countermove in response to Adam and Eve's actions; Jesus was the plan from the very beginning, even before Genesis 1:1.

The Fall of man was part of God's design from the outset. It was a detail God didn't leave to chance. If so, that could have been quite a blow to God's omnipotence if God had planned all along for Jesus only to have it play out another way. I mean, if Adam and Eve hadn't eaten from the forbidden fruit, there would have been no need for Jesus. Thankfully, God micromanaged then, just as it is to this day. Jesus says in Matthew 10:29-31,

> Are not two sparrows sold for a copper coin? And not one
> of them falls to the ground apart from your Father's will.
> But the very hairs of your head are numbered. Do not fear
> therefore; you are of more value than many sparrows.

We can see from that text that God clearly is in the details. If not one bird falls from the sky apart from His design and every hair on everyone's head is numbered, I'd say that God is a micromanager, wouldn't you?

A Micromanaged Plan

Now let's look at God's role in your salvation. I saw a sign outside a church recently that read, "God is waiting for you to accept Jesus. What are you waiting for?" I snapped a picture of it and often use it in my seminars. The critical question is whether it is true. If God is waiting on you to do anything, then one could argue who is really sovereign. If God is waiting on you to make a decision, then that paints a picture of a passive, sometimes helpless God. If God is waiting on you to make a decision, it stands to reason that someone might choose to reject Jesus, thus thwarting God's plan.

The truth is, God is not waiting on you for anything. God orchestrated the ends and the means. You believe in Jesus because it was God's plan for you to do so. You're right, I do believe in predestination, but please note that I didn't invent the word. It is straight out of Scripture. I won't list all the passages that talk of us being predestined, but Paul wrote extensively on the subject. In Ephesians 1:4-5 he wrote,

> He chose us in Him before the foundation of the world, that we should be holy and without blame before Him in love, having predestined us to adoption as sons by Jesus Christ to Himself according to the good pleasure of His will.

Here we should note that God chose us to be in Christ before the foundation of the world. Again, this happened before Genesis 1:1.

In Ephesians 1:11 Paul continues, "In Him also we have obtained an inheritance, being predestined according to the purpose of Him who works all things according to the counsel of His will." We were chosen because it was God's will.

Were we chosen because God knew we would choose Him? If that were the case, God could conceivably be waiting to bestow His love on us. However, that's not what Scripture says. Turn to 1 John 4:19 for the answer, "We love Him because He first loved us." That's pretty clear. He doesn't love us because we chose Jesus, He loves us because we belonged to Him before the foundation of the world. We love Jesus because God loved us first. We love because God loved.

Perhaps the strongest text in the Bible to support predestination is found in John 1:12-13:

> As many as received Him, to them He gave the right to become children of God, to those who believe in His name [so far it sounds as if we do the choosing, but let's continue]: who were born not of blood, nor of the will of the flesh, nor of the will of man, but of God.

To me, it's as plain as day. It's not of bloodlines, not of our own will, but that of God. That may elicit different reactions in different people, but as for me, I find tremendous comfort. It's not up to me. It's up to God. If my salvation were left in my hands, I'm not sure I could rest. I'd always be second-guessing myself and wondering if there was more I could do. I can't speak for anyone else, but I am thankful that God is a control freak!

> If my salvation were left in my hands, I'm not sure I could rest. I'd always be second-guessing myself and wondering if there was more I could do.

God Calls, You Come

One final passage to hopefully make my case is Romans 8:29. I turn to this passage because some might still be confusing foreknowledge and predestination. They are distinctly different as Romans 8:29-30 explains:

> Whom He foreknew, He also predestined to be conformed to the image of His Son, that He might be the firstborn among many brethren. Moreover whom He predestined, these He also called; whom He called, these He also justified; and whom He justified, these He also glorified.

This is sometimes referred to as the "Golden Chain of Salvation."

First God predestined, then He called, then He justifies, then He glorifies. It gives us the order and it clearly distinguishes between foreknowledge and predestination.

Which leads us to another burning question, Can we resist the call? It's one thing to be predestined, but can we choose to resist? I will cover this answer more extensively in the next chapter, but for now let me say loudly and boldly, *no*. Like all details, that is yet another critical detail that God didn't leave to chance.

I like to use good old-fashioned logic on this point. It is written in John 6:65, and this is Jesus speaking: "No one can come to Me unless it has been granted to him by My Father." That says to me that we can't choose Jesus unless it is God's will for us to do so, and if it is God's will, it is inconceivable to me that God would leave the most important part to chance. That is, the coming! If God calls and potentially we may not come, then His call is subject to our actions, thus making us more sovereign than God. The thankful truth is that when God calls, we go!

An awesome story of the power of God's call is the story of Lazarus, which is found in John 11. I'll recap the story. Lazarus fell deathly ill and his friends went to tell Jesus. Jesus answered that his sickness would not end in death and they were relieved. Of course, Jesus was talking about spiritual death, not physical death. It was only a couple days later that Jesus informed them that He knew Lazarus was actually dead. So, they traveled to Bethany to pay respects to Lazarus. By the time they arrived, Lazarus had been dead for four days, and his body was decaying. Jesus ordered that the tombstone be removed and called out, "Lazarus, come forth!" Imagine the looks on everyone's face as Jesus stood outside the tomb and called for a dead man to respond. However, just moments later, Lazarus walked out as alive as he could be. Lazarus could not have resisted the call any more than anyone else. When the voice of God calls, we will respond.

Running Amuck for God?

Finally, I want to examine the role of God in day-to-day life. It stands to reason that if God has called you to believe in Jesus, God must have a plan for you. Another popular saying I heard many years ago (and mentioned previously in this book) is, "What you are is God's gift to you, what you make of yourself is your gift to God." I even considered making that saying its own chapter of this book. It basically says that God creates you and then takes a passive role to see what you do with your life. It also implies that we must work to try and pay God back for what He's done for us.

That may sound good, but both interpretations are far from the truth. God doesn't sit back and hope you do the things He has planned, He directs your steps. Before you get to thinking that my words may be a bit strong, look at Proverbs 16:9, "A man's heart plans his way, but the LORD directs his steps." One of the most important truths we can discover is that God has a plan for everyone. That plan is different for everyone but we all have a singular, central theme: to serve God.

Fellow author, and pastor, Rick Warren writes in his mega-best-selling book *The Purpose-Driven Life* that we were created, saved, and called to serve God. We do that in countless different ways, with countless different gifts, but we are here to serve God. Some will do it through community service, others by corporate work and creating jobs, some by medical service, others by keeping the civil peace, some by tending to the earth's natural resources, others by being a good friend or parent. No job on earth is more significant or more impor-tant than another. The world may place status on our roles, but we're all just body parts contributing together to serve God.

Paul wrote about this in 1 Corinthians 12. The entire chapter 12 is devoted to talking about our individual gifts and how we all work together for the glory of God, but allow me to pick out a few passages to illustrate this truth. Verses 4 through 6 say,

> There are diversities of gifts, but the same Spirit. There are differences of ministries, but the same Lord. And there are diversities of activities, but it is the same God who works all in all.

Notice who does the working? God. And what does He work? All in all.

Verse 12 says, "As the body is one and has many members, but all the members of that one body, being many, are one body, so also is Christ." Paul goes on to say that every body part is just as important as the next. In fact, he writes in verse 22 that many parts which appear to be weaker are just the opposite. Our own bodies are excellent illustrations of how we all move and serve one purpose. Our arms and legs may do most of the work, but how much would they get done without our fingers? How much can we do without our eyes? What if everything operated perfectly except a small sliver of our brains that controls movement and makes possible what our arms can do? How useful would our legs be without the small ligaments in our knees?

Every body part has a function and every part works together for our overall welfare. All things and all parts work together for God's purpose. I talked about that in an earlier chapter, but here we see how our own individual gifts play a role in God's overall plan. How often have we been distressed that something happened, only to be thankful later in life that it did? The old proverb is true, "Too soon old, too late smart." Life lessons give us wisdom, and as we grow older we realize how little we knew when we were younger. Guess what—when we come face-to-face with God, we will in turn realize how little we knew on earth. We can find peace in knowing that God knows and that He works in everyone and uses every gift for a greater good we won't understand this side of heaven.

A word of caution, however. Don't think for a moment that God doesn't use infirmities every bit as much as He uses strengths. Don't think for a moment that every body part has to be completely healthy and working the way everyone thinks it should to have a purpose in serving God. Some of the most shining examples of God's grace and love can be found in people with what the world would call disabilities. As I stated earlier in the chapter about angels, one of the greatest Bible teachers I have ever met lived in poverty and was confined to a bed.

You've heard the phrase, "God didn't make no junk," and God

didn't make any accidents. There isn't a single person on the face of the planet that wasn't created by God for a purpose. For some, our purpose may seem evident. For others, we may not know what that purpose was until we reach our next life. In 2 Timothy 1:9 it is written that we were called by a holy calling given to us before time began. As believers, we were set apart, saved, and called by a holy calling. We all have a purpose, and God works in us to accomplish that purpose. In 1 Thessalonians 5:24, Paul writes, "He who calls you is faithful, who also will do it." God doesn't call you to something you cannot accomplish. He calls you to do what you were meant to do and then directs your steps in getting it done.

God is not a hands-off God. He is in control of every detail from the very beginning. He left nothing to chance. If even the smallest of details was left to chance, then there is a possibility things wouldn't go as God had wanted them to go. Thankfully, the truth is that God *is* a micromanager. He is in control, and He likes it that way. The end has already been written, and we should find total peace and comfort that God has it all figured out.

It is written in Hebrews 4:10, "He who has entered His rest has himself also ceased from his works as God did from His." God's work is done and that means *your* work is also done. You're still playing it out, because we are still bound by earthly time, but to God, it is done, as confirmed by the words of Paul in Ephesians 2:8-10:

> By grace you have been saved through faith and that not of yourselves; it is the gift of God, not of works, lest anyone should boast. For we are His workmanship, created in Christ Jesus for good works, which God prepared beforehand that we should walk in them.

Amen to that.

GOD IS NOT A MICROMANAGER • EVERYONE HAS THEIR OWN FREE WILL • THERE AR ROADS TO HEAVEN • WHEN WE DIE WE BECOME ANGELS • GOD HELPS THOSE WHO HEL SELVES • GOD WANTS YOU TO BE RICH • CHRISTIANS AREN'T PERFECT, JUST FORGIVEN RE GOD'S CO-PILOTS • PRAY HARD AND GOD WILL ANSWER • GOD AND SATAN ARE BATTLIN T • GOD IS NOT A MICROMANAGER • EVERYONE HAS THEIR OWN FREE WILL • THERE AR ROADS TO HEAVEN • WHEN WE D ANGELS • GOD HELPS THOSE WHO HEL SELVES • GOD WANTS YOU TO BE RICH • CHRISTIANS AREN'T PERFECT, JUST FORGIVEN RE GOD'S CO-PILOTS • PRAY HARD AND GOD WILL ANSWER

CHAPTER 11

BELIEF #10

Everyone Has Their Own Free Will

This is the mother of all popular beliefs and the one that causes the most debate. In fact, almost every one of the preceding popular beliefs has its roots in the belief that everyone has their own free will. I've hinted at this in many preceding chapters, but I decided I should tackle it head-on in the final chapter. Perhaps no belief is as sacred to us as believing we have a free will. My experience tells me that most people are open to a lot of new truths, but when it comes to free will, we're as closed as a bank vault.

As I stated in the introduction, my intention is not necessarily to cause you to agree with everything I write about, but rather to cause you to study for yourself. This is no exception. Don't accept something as being true just because you've heard it your entire life. The world believes many things that aren't in the Bible, and the world believes many things that later have been proven to not be true. It was common wisdom just a few hundred years ago that rotting meat actually turned into maggots, then into flies. If a book came out in that era claiming otherwise, it would have been immediately dismissed as baloney. So keep an open mind. You've made it this far and you haven't put the book down. Maybe there's a greater reason for buying and reading this book. Just hang with me.

I have three contentions to explore in this chapter and, as I have throughout this book, I will support my assertions with Scripture.

1. I contend that believing we have a free will is the ultimate condition of our humanity.

2. We often confuse making choices with free will.

3. As believers, we exchanged a free will for a will that is bonded and fused with Christ.

First, let's look at why we so desperately cling to the idea of free will. Believing in, and ultimately having, free will is a direct result of the curse of the Garden. Let me explain. Most people argue that Adam and Eve had a free will and as a result of their having a free will, they chose to eat the forbidden fruit. I believe it was the other way around. I believe they didn't start out with a free will, but later got it as a result of eating the forbidden fruit and sin entering the world.

Adam and Eve were created to be "one" with God. There was no need for a separate free will. They had everything and walked with the Lord every day. Their will was God's will. If Adam and Eve really did have a free will, it is at least theoretically possible they could have chosen *not* to be tempted by Satan and *not* to eat the fruit, thus making the need for Jesus and a redemptive plan obsolete. That would have forced God into a reactive role. That would have made God go to Plan B.

> Adam and Eve didn't surprise God. He created them and knew what they would do.

Thankfully, as we've hopefully already established, God is not a reactive God. He alone is sovereign, and in light of the fact that in Revelation 13:8, it is written that the Lamb was slain before the foundation of the world, God had the plan to redeem people long before He ever created Adam and Eve. So, with that being the case, Adam and Eve must have done exactly what God had planned for them to do. Sure, God was disappointed in the sense that He never likes sin, but Adam and Eve didn't surprise God. He created them and knew what they would do, because it was in His plan.

Is Free Will Better?

Free will entered when sin entered. Note the tree that held the forbidden fruit was not the Tree of Good and Evil, it was the Tree of the *Knowledge* of Good and Evil. Evil didn't enter the world when Satan showed up—evil must have always been there. Adam and Eve just didn't know about it. Notice the lie that Satan used to tempt them. Satan played to their humanity. Satan told them that if they ate the beautiful fruit, they too could be like God. Satan played to their vanity.

Of course, when they had partaken of the fruit, they became separated from God.[1] This was the fall of man. It was this "separation" that gave them their own free will. They were now free to do exactly what their will wanted to do, and that was to choose sin. This is what is meant when Paul wrote in Romans 3:10-18. In verses 10 through 12 he declares,

> There is none righteous, no not one; There is none who understands; There is none who seeks after God. They all have turned aside; They have together become unprofitable; There is none who does good, no, not one.

This describes our human condition. We are born spiritually dead. We are born dead in our trespasses, as Paul writes in Ephesians 2:1. In this condition, we can't help but sin because it is who we are. Our natural state is unrighteous.

I believe unbelievers still have a free will. We know this is true by reading Romans 1:18-32. I suggest reading and studying the full text, but here's a snippet (verses 24-26):

> God also gave them up to uncleanness, in the lusts of their hearts, to dishonor their bodies among themselves, who

exchanged the truth of God for the lie, and worshipped and
served the creature rather than the Creator, who is blessed
forever. Amen. For this reason God gave them up to vile
passions.

Adam and Eve exchanged the truth for a lie, and God gave them up
to their vile passions. They got a free will.

Believers, on the other hand, have been rescued. We've been saved.
We exchanged our "old dead man" for a new creation in Christ. There
are many biblical references to the old man and the new man, but let's
look at Ephesians 4:22-24, which teaches "that you put off, concerning your former conduct, the old man which grows corrupt according
to the deceitful lusts, and be renewed in the spirit of your mind, and
that you put on the new man which was created according to God,
in true righteousness and holiness."

I also like 1 Corinthians 15:46-49, that says, as believers, we once
were like Adam, but now we're like Jesus. Believers have been born
again and are new creations in Christ. The phrase "in Christ," means
just that. We now have the spirit and mind of Christ.[2] The Bible also
refers to being born again as being "bought" by God, in 1 Corinthians
6:20, and 1 Corinthians 7:23. We don't belong to Satan anymore; we
belong to God. Those who have not been born again still belong to
Satan.

We can see a biblical example of this in John 8:44-47, when Jesus
told a group of Pharisees, "You are of your father the devil," and in verse
47, "Therefore you do not hear, because you are not of God." Thus,
anyone who is of God has exchanged the will that doesn't know Him
for one that does. Sure, we have a will, but our will is dictated by our
nature. Before we were saved we had a sinful nature and thus our will
loved to sin. Once we have been saved and are in Christ, we no longer
have a sinful nature and although we still sin in the flesh, we repent
and feel remorse when we do that which is against our nature.

Now here's where the confusion comes in. We make choices every
day and we seem free enough when we make them. It is because we

feel that way that we conclude we have free will. No one is putting a gun to your head when you "choose" to eat at that restaurant, wear that shirt, or see that movie. There's no doubt we make choices every day and our choices seem to be free—but are they? I contend that even though we experience making choices, our steps are pre-ordained. I've already cited such passages as Ephesians 2:10 and Proverbs 16:9, but let's look at a few more.

How about Jeremiah 10:23, "O LORD, I know the way of man is not in himself; it is not in man who walks to direct his own steps." Another great passage is Philippians 2:13: "It is God who works in you both to will and to do for His good pleasure." There are many other passages but in those it is clearly written that God directs our steps. It is God who works in us to will *and* to do. We feel like we're making free choices, but God is guiding us every step of the way. The operative word is *feel*. We *feel* free and we experience the act of making a choice, but God is working in us to will and to do.

How Free Can You Be?

The other operative word in the whole free-will debate is the word *free*. It's a powerful word. In advertising and marketing, "free" has proven to be a very effective lure. Our entire system of government is based on "free" rights. We cherish our independence and take pride that we live in a "free" nation. The word is very emotional to us. Clearly, democratic countries such as the United States may be freer than many other countries, but we're far from completely free. We're not free to do whatever we want.

And let's look a bit closer at the facts. Are we free to fly? Could you stand on the edge of a mountain, flap your arms, and fly like a bird? No. You are not free to fly. Are you free to heal yourself? If you have some condition or disease, can you snap your fingers and instantly be cured? No. You are not free to heal yourself. Are you free to choose the country you were born in? Are you free to select your skin color or intelligence? The answer is no and no. This answer is also found in the Bible in Jeremiah 13:23, "Can the Ethiopian change his skin or the leopard its spots?" The biblical answer is no. We are not free to determine our lot in life. That is God's choosing and His alone.

Are you free to drive down the freeway at 120 miles per hour? No. We may be thrown in jail. Are we free to yell "fire" in a crowded theater? No—we may get put in handcuffs. Certain things are out of our control and certain things bind us due to the law. Either way, we are not completely free.

Now, you might be saying that we might not be free to fly but we are most free to drive as fast as we want or yell "fire" in a crowded theater. We don't have the ability to fly, but we have the ability to drive recklessly. You'd be right. So do it. I'll bet that even though you may have the ability to drive recklessly, you don't. I'll bet it's because you don't want to. You choose not to.

That is my point. As a Christian, you don't want to commit murder, because it is no longer your nature to sin. That doesn't mean you will never sin; it just means it is no longer consistent with who you are. If you were really free, you wouldn't even consider the consequences. You would just act on instinct, and you certainly wouldn't feel any remorse. The truth is, we're only as free as our conscience will allow.

Let me put it another way—we're only as free as God allows. We're free in Christ, not free in our humanity. We have free grace, not free will. Your sinful nature and free will were replaced with that of Christ's. You now have His nature. You now have the mind of Christ and are one spirit with Him.[3] God has worked in you so that you no longer have the will to sin or break the law. You still have the ability, and your flesh will still do so, but you don't like it and feel bad when you do. It isn't who you are anymore.

Free Will Isn't All It's Cracked Up to Be

This all leads us to the objection I hear more than any other: the "puppet" objection. Most people argue that it sounds like I am saying that we are nothing more than God's puppet. Well, I am. The difference is, I am saying it like this: "Yes, we are free. We belong to God," instead of like this: "We're mindless puppets. We can do nothing on our own." I celebrate God being in charge instead of me being in charge. I am happy to be a slave in Christ. The truth is that we are all a slave to something. We are all a puppet to someone. We are either a puppet of Satan or a puppet of Christ. You choose. (And the kicker is, even puppets of Satan are puppets of God! They just have no clue.)

I don't want free will because that would mean I would still belong to the world. That would mean I wouldn't have been bought by God, as written in 1 Corinthians 7:23, and it would mean I wouldn't have been born anew.

Ironically, free will is not so desirable. Paul wrote in Galatians 6:3, "For if anyone thinks himself to be something, when he is nothing, he deceives himself." Believing in free will is the ultimate tool of the devil because it exalts man and lowers God. Paul knew this and it came through in all his writings. Paul knew that whatever exalted man, lowered God.

Paul took delight in being Christ's slave. He began a couple of his letters in the New Testament by identifying himself as "Paul, a bondservant of Jesus." For those who may not know the difference between a servant and a bondservant, a bondservant is one who can never be anything else. Regular servants can eventually earn their freedom—a bondservant cannot.

Paul also knew that having his own free will was not what the world thought it was. Paul knew that if not having his own free will was good enough for Jesus, it was good enough for him. Jesus repeated in many passages how He didn't come to do His will but instead that of the Father. In Philippians 2:5-7 Paul wrote about this:

> Let this mind be in you which was also in Christ Jesus, who, being in the form of God, did not consider it robbery to be equal to God, but made Himself of no reputation, taking the form of a bondservant, and coming in the likeness of men.

Even Jesus was a bondservant, but the line we should not gloss over is that Jesus did not consider it "robbery" to be equal to God.

Too many Christians, in my opinion, cling to free will and act as if it's highway robbery to even remotely consider not having it. On the most important eve of His life, Jesus wanted a different outcome. Jesus prayed, "Abba, Father, all things are possible for You. Take this cup away from Me; nevertheless, not what I will, but what You will" (Mark 14:36). Jesus wanted a different fate, but God had a different plan. How often is that the case for us? We think we know what we want, but ultimately God knows better. Jesus also knew He wasn't free to choose what He wanted. He knew He didn't have free will. If Jesus didn't have free will, what makes us think we do?

□ □ □

This debate didn't begin here, and it certainly won't end here. I know I have not made the definitive case against free will, but perhaps I have jump-started you into exploring it further. Again, I stand with Martin Luther. Back in 1525, he wrote a book called *The Bondage of the Will*, which was a rebuttal of a book by the theologian Erasmus titled *The Freedom of the Will*. Erasmus exalted free will, while Luther ascribed all freedom and power to God and total dependency to man.

> As Augustine once wrote, "A man's free will...avails for nothing except to sin, if he knows not the way of truth."

Luther's last recorded words on his deathbed, on February 18, 1546, were, "Wir sind bettler. Hoc est verum," which means "We are beggars. This is true." Luther knew that man is utterly helpless and that God is our only source of strength. He continually argued that God gets all the glory and we get all His grace.

This is the true resting point of grace and peace. As long as we cling to even the slightest shred of credit and autonomy, God doesn't get 100 percent of the glory. John Piper, in his excellent book *The Legacy of Sovereign Joy,* writes, "Grace is the key because it is free and creates a new heart with delights that govern the will and the work of our lives." The more I study, the more convinced I am that grace is indeed the key. That is why I believe in free grace, not free will. As Augustine once wrote,

> A man's free will, indeed, avails for nothing except to sin, if he knows not the way of truth; and even after his duty and his proper aim shall begin to become known to him, unless he also take delight in and feel a love for it, he neither does his duty, nor sets about it, nor lives rightly. Now, in order that such a course may engage our affections, God's love is shed abroad in our hearts not through the free will which arises from ourselves, but through the Holy Ghost, which is given to us.[4]

That's amazing grace!

Thus, grace is the only thing we should boast in because it shines the light of credit where it needs to be. Paul again says it best, in Galatians 6:14: God forbid that I should boast except in the cross of our Lord Jesus Christ, by whom the world has been crucified to me, and I to the world." No need to boast in our individuality any longer. As a believer, you now belong entirely and exclusively to God.

GOD IS NOT A MICROMANAGER • EVERYONE HAS THEIR OWN FREE WILL • THERE AR
ROADS TO HEAVEN • WHEN WE DIE WE BECOME ANGELS • GOD HELPS THOSE WHO HEL
SELVES • GOD WANTS YOU TO BE RICH • CHRISTIANS AREN'T PERFECT, JUST FORGIVEN •
E GOD'S CO-PILOTS • PRAY HARD AND GOD WILL ANSWER • GOD AND SATAN ARE BATTLIN
T • GOD IS NOT A MICROMANAGER • EVERYONE HAS THEIR OWN FREE WILL • THERE AR
ROADS TO HEAVEN • WHEN WE DIE WE BECOME ANGELS • GOD HELPS THOSE WHO HEL
SELVES • GOD WANTS YOU TO BE RICH • CHRISTIANS AREN'T PERFECT, JUST FORGIVEN

Why God's
Truth Is Better

HARD AND GOD WILL ANSWER • GOD AND SATAN ARE BATTLING IT OUT • GOD IS NOT A M
ANAGER • EVERYONE HAS THEIR OWN FREE WILL • THERE ARE MANY ROADS TO HEAVEN
WE DIE WE BECOME ANGELS • GOD HELPS THOSE WHO HELP THEMSELVES • GOD WANT
TO BE RICH • CHRISTIANS AREN'T PERFECT, JUST FORGIVEN • WE ARE GOD'S CO-PILOTS
HARD AND GOD WILL ANSWER • GOD AND SATAN ARE BATTLING IT OUT • GOD IS NOT A M
ANAGER • EVERYONE HAS THEIR OWN FREE WILL • THERE ARE MANY ROADS TO HEAVEN
WE DIE WE BECOME ANGELS • GOD HELPS THOSE WHO HELP THEMSELVES • GOD WAN
TO BE RICH • CHRISTIANS AREN'T PERFECT, JUST FORGIVEN • WE ARE GOD'S CO-PILOTS

GOD IS NOT A MICROMANAGER • EVERYONE HAS THEIR OWN FREE WILL • THERE ARE
ROADS TO HEAVEN • WHEN WE DIE WE BECOME ANGELS • GOD HELPS THOSE WHO HELP
ELVES • GOD WANTS YOU TO BE RICH • CHRISTIANS AREN'T PERFECT, JUST FORGIVEN •
GOD'S CO-PILOTS • PRAY HARD AND GOD WILL ANSWER • GOD AND SATAN ARE BATTLING
• GOD IS NOT A MICROMANAGER • EVERYONE HAS THEIR OWN FREE WILL • THERE ARE
ROADS TO HEAVEN • WHEN WE DIE WE BECOME ANGELS • GOD HELPS THOSE WHO HELP
ELVES • GOD WANTS YOU TO BE RICH • CHRISTIANS AREN'T PERFECT, JUST FORGIVEN •
GOD'S CO-PILOTS • PRAY HARD AND GOD WILL ANSWER •

CHAPTER 12

Another Reformation

In this final chapter there are a couple lingering questions I'd like to address. First, there's the question about why finding biblical truth is so critical, and second, where religion could be heading. I believe both questions are intertwined and lead to the same destination. And that, I believe, is another reformation.

Preceding the great Reformation sparked most prominently by Martin Luther, biblical truth had become obscured and distorted. Organized religion had become big business, and the Bible had lost its central place. Luther's protest came out of Luther's love for Scripture and the burning need he felt to get back to what it says. Luther believed and argued that the Bible was the living Word of God, the means He ordained for both believers and unbelievers to find Him and His truth.* Luther felt the world had gotten to a place where people took the word of man over the Word of God. He felt religion had gotten too big, too corrupt, and had too much power. The words of the religious leaders at that time were hailed as truth, regardless of whether or not they sprang from Scripture. If it was said in church, it must be truth. Bits and pieces of the Bible were twisted to fit whatever the prevailing thought of the day was.

---

* If you accept this as God's plan for the Bible, then believing in its accurate preservation through the genera-tions is a mere minor technicality. God created life and all of the heavens and the earth. Preserving His Word is certainly within His ability.

This is where I believe we are today. We believe what feels right to us instead of what *is* right. We believe what sounds logical and popular instead of consulting the Bible. People spend more time in church than they do reading and studying God's Word. (Don't misunderstand me. Going to church is a good thing, but it should not be a substitute for knowing the Bible.) We remember what the preacher said but don't know what God said. We can quote our Sunday school teacher but can't quote Paul. If all this sounds a bit alarmist, let me give you a few more specific examples. Here's a quick quiz.

Who said the immortal words of history, "I have a dream?" Did you recognize those words as being from Martin Luther King Jr.? Who said, "Give me liberty or give me death?" You might not have known they were the words of Patrick Henry, but you knew they came from the time of the American Revolution. How about, "Ask not what your country can do for you; ask what you can do for your country." You probably knew they were from President Kennedy. The sad truth is, we know more words from man than we do from God.

We celebrate and teach the language in the Declaration of Independence and Bill of Rights, but the language in the Ten Commandments is off limits. We can recite the Pledge of Allegiance, but can't recite the words of the Sermon on the Mount. In fact, most believers do not even know where to find Jesus' Sermon on the Mount.[1]

We know the story of the "Three Little Pigs," but don't know the story of the rich young ruler. We know the intimate details of Santa Claus and the poem "'Twas the Night Before Christmas," but don't know the intimate details of the star of Bethlehem. We know the life story of our favorite sports star, but don't know the story of Paul's conversion on the road to Damascus. We know the phrase "In God We Trust" only because it's on our money. In practice, we trust the words of others way before we consult and trust the Word of God. You get the idea. We know so little of what really matters!

We're Stuck on Labels

Now I may not be talking about you specifically, but I am talking about the state of religion as a whole. We need to get back to the Bible and absolute truth. We need to fall in love with it again, just as Luther did. We need another reformation. Most people don't know that every Protestant denomination has its roots in the Reformation. The word *Protestant* came from the word *protest*. The Reformation was a protest. If you are a Methodist, Baptist, Lutheran, Episcopalian, or Presbyterian, the roots of your church can be traced to one of the great Reformers or their heirs. They all believed the Bible and the Bible alone. No added spin or emphasis needed. If you are nondenominational, your sole source for truth and wisdom should be the Bible. If you're Catholic, even St. Peter is right now pointing directly at Jesus and the words of Scripture, not at any man.

I believe wholeheartedly that denomination division is man-made. Paul warned about this when he wrote in verse 10 of 1 Corinthians 1:10-17,

> I plead with you brethren, by the name of our Lord Jesus Christ, that you all speak the same thing and that there be no divisions among you, but that you be perfectly joined together in the same mind and in the same judgment.

He went on to say that Christ was being divided and truth was being distorted. Teachers of the Word were getting famous. Teachers of the Word were getting more credit than God.

This is where we too have landed. We can name more TV evangelists than we can authors of Scripture! As best as anyone can estimate, we now have over 34,000 separate Christian groups in the world.[2] It is projected that by the year 2020, we will have over 50,000 recognized denominations. Indeed, religion has become more complicated, fragmented, and a bigger business than ever before, but what that tells me even more is that we are mixing, matching, and molding truth to fit what we want to believe. We need more and more denominations to keep pace with individual belief systems.

With that said, I do understand how labels get created. We live in a world that loves labels and easy ways to define people. Somewhere along the way saying you are a Christian has become like saying you are an American. Being an American doesn't describe someone enough. We want to know where they live, where they were born, what they do for a living, and so on. We're defined more for what we do for a living than what we believe. Saying you're a Christian has become way too vague.

When people ask me what I believe, I try to get away with saying I'm a believer in Christ and believe in the Bible, but rarely does that satisfy the questioner. They ask me where I go to church and what denomination and category of religious belief do I subscribe to. I fought this for years. I argued that being a believer should be a sufficient answer, but people just thought that I said that because I either didn't know anything beyond that or didn't have deep convictions on the matter. Some even questioned my faith.

Then I said I was nondenominational. I used to say the Bible was my denomination. That seemed to be satisfactory to most, but it often got interpreted as that I don't have a church home. And if a believer doesn't have a church home, then they must be a rebel or a troublemaker.

My Challenge to You

Well, I must confess that I delight in challenging people's belief systems, so to that end, I've come up with another answer to the question of what I believe when simply being a "believer" isn't enough. I've come up with my own label (which I already mentioned at the beginning of this book). I call myself a "sovereignist" and I believe in "sovereignism." I like using those terms because it always leads to more questions and I get a chance to explain what they mean. I use many ways to define Sovereignism, but the one I use most often simply defines it as "All God. All the time." It's catchy, but it's the truth. God has been in charge of everything since before the world began and He will reign supreme forever and ever.

This captures parts of a lot of belief systems. I believe God created the world and everything in it, so one could call me a Creationist. I believe in the inerrancy and absoluteness of the Bible, so that might make me a Fundamentalist. I believe in spreading the good news of Jesus as we are called and that might make an Evangelical. I believe in predestination, so that might make me a Calvinist.

I know I've painted with a broad brush, but my point is valid. We have too many labels and too many divisions, but I'm no different.

People are searching. I see it in their eyes when I speak...People want and need God, even if they don't completely realize it yet.

We take bits and pieces and form them together to make up our own personal belief system. We need another reformation. I believe the next reformation will be a movement back to basics, as was the first. I believe we need to get back to God and His Word. That's why I love the label Sovereignism. If we must label ourselves, let's give God all the credit, all the glory, and fall in love with His Word. *Sovereignism is the acknowledgement and celebration of God being God.*

So, "What's the harm?" someone asked me one time. "It's a free world and faith is a personal issue. What someone believes is what someone believes." This also is a popular position. Individuality is the mantra of the day. The problem is, we're losing truth. As stated earlier and in the beginning chapters of this book, popularity is trumping truth and it's time to take a stand. I believe people are craving real, life-changing truth. I believe people are desperately seeking real peace and joy in their lives. I believe people want to believe in things deeply and passionately. I believe people need hope and inspiration like never before. I believe deep down that people want to know that there is someone much bigger and more powerful than we are, someone who has everything under control. And I believe that people want happy endings.

People are searching. I see it in their eyes when I speak. I read the stories every day. People want and need God, even if they don't completely realize it yet. And—drumroll, please—all of this and more is ours for the taking. It's all in the Holy Bible! We're all in the hands of a sovereign God. That is absolute truth. There are no degrees of sovereignty, no different ways to interpret it, no individual definitions, no personal twist, just plain biblical truth!

I know that seems bold sometimes, and perhaps I've even taken you aback a time or two in your reading of this book. I can assure you that my only motivation in doing so comes from a love for the truth and what it's done in my life. In the ten years since I was confronted with some of the shocking truths of the Bible, they have completely changed my life. My life hasn't been any easier—things still don't always go as I want them to go, and I still have my share of trials and tribulations. The difference is, I now understand that God is in charge and has a plan. I might not like it or understand it but I can now rest in the fact that it's the way God wants it to be.

I sincerely hope you've found something in this book that will cause you to dive back into God's Word. Perhaps it's to find something to prove me wrong. Perhaps it's just to learn more, or maybe just because it's been awhile since you've seen what the Bible has to say. Whatever the reason, it's a good one. Don't accept popular belief just because it's popular and you've heard it all your life. I can assure you that the truth in Scripture is far more life-changing, peace-delivering, and inspiring than anything a mere human might say. But you've got to discover that for yourself.

Martin Luther once wrote, "It's a sin and shame not to know our own book or to understand the speech and words of our God." We know the words of the world—it's the right time now to know what *God* has to say. I invite and challenge you to become a Sovereignist and spread the word of what that means. You never know—maybe God will use you as we move toward another great reformation of His church. Give God all the glory and then, *and only then,* will you experience all His grace.

GOD IS NOT A MICROMANAGER • EVERYONE HAS THEIR OWN FREE WILL • THERE ARE
ROADS TO HEAVEN • WHEN WE DIE WE BECOME ANGELS • GOD HELPS THOSE WHO HELP
ELVES • GOD WANTS YOU TO BE RICH • CHRISTIANS AREN'T PERFECT, JUST FORGIVEN •
E GOD'S CO-PILOTS • PRAY HARD AND GOD WILL ANSWER • GOD AND SATAN ARE BATTLING
• GOD IS NOT A MICROMANAGER • EVERYONE HAS THEIR OWN FREE WILL • THERE ARE
ROADS TO HEAVEN • WHEN WE DIE WE BECOME ANGELS • GOD HELPS THOSE WHO HELP
ELVES • GOD WANTS YOU TO BE RICH • CHRISTIANS AREN'T PERFECT, JUST FORGIVEN •
E GOD'S CO-PILOTS • PRAY HARD AND GOD WILL ANSWER • GOD FOR SATAN ARE BATTLING

AN AFTERTHOUGHT FROM THE AUTHOR

Beyond the Beliefs

If I've succeeded in my mission, you are more than likely thinking one of three things. The first possibility is that you're not shocked about what you've read, because you've either encountered these things before or they are totally in line with what you already believe. If that's the case, praise God and continue spreading the good news about the life-changing truths of the Bible.

Maybe You Have Concerns and Questions

The second possibility is that you're thinking and feeling apprehensive. You agree with some things and disagree with others. Some of my arguments sound convincing, but you're just not sure. After all, some of the things I've written about may be completely contrary to what you've believed all your life. If this is you, you're not alone. In fact, some readers may even be a bit riled up. That's okay. It may be the Holy Spirit pressing you to be clear as to what you do believe. As I stated in the introduction, my only goal is to drive you to the Word. I don't have all the answers, but God's Word does.

I'll always remember the time I met my friend Charles Gwin. For many years, Charles owned and singlehandedly operated a small Christian bookstore, called The Gathering Place, in my hometown. He was a friend to many people, and his small shop doubled as a counseling clinic for the patrons who wandered into the store.

One day, the Lord directed me to him. After an hour of talking about God, I convinced Charles to allow me to conduct a Bible course one night a week in his shop. I called it "The Grace Course." (Most of the material for my two books has been taken and distilled from that program.)

Anyway, I'll never forget the night of the very first session. It was attended by a dozen or so people. Charles included. As I went through some of my introductory material, I noticed him fidgeting in his chair. I couldn't tell whether he was nervous, agitated, or both. By the time I completed my "Grace Course Quiz," I had my answer. Charles was mad. He had enough. He stood up and, in no uncertain terms, let me know what he thought.

Although I can't recall the exact words he used, I do clearly remember him telling me I didn't know what I was talking about. Charles was a man of the Word. He owned a Christian bookstore. He was a deacon in his church. He wore a cross around his neck. He was a pillar of the community. He knew everyone, and hundreds of people visited his store on a regular basis just so they could pray with him. He knew the Bible well, or so he thought. Some other attendees also chimed in. Others just froze in stunned silence when Charles suggested it might be best to call an end to the course right then and there.

I remember a long, tension-filled pause. What I said next is a blur in my memory, but whatever it was, it calmed things down enough to allow me to proceed. Both Charles and I have since tried to recall what it was that I said, but we can't. That reminds me of the story in Exodus 4 when God called Moses to lead the people of Israel out of Egypt. In verse 10, Moses pleads to God that he isn't the right person for the job. He says, "I am not eloquent, neither before nor since You have spoken to Your servant; but I am slow of speech and slow of tongue." God's reply is awesome. In the very next verse, the Lord answered, "Who has made man's mouth? Now therefore, go, and I will be with your mouth and teach you what you shall say."

I love that passage. It is yet another example of God's sovereignty. We think we control our mouths, but it was God who made mouths and will give us the words we need when we need them. I believe that night in The Gathering Place, God gave me the words to defuse the tense situation so the course could go on.

To jump ahead, the course grew in numbers and was repeated many times over. As for Charles, he and I are now good friends. Like me when I first heard some of the truths I've written about, he dove headfirst into the Bible to challenge my assertions. But the more he studied, the more he saw God's providence and grace. Charles thanks me for opening his eyes to God's incredible grace and sovereignty, but we both know where the credit really belongs. He has since sold his bookstore, but he continues to sell Christian books wholesale and never misses an opportunity to share the amazing truths of the Bible with anyone who even remotely asks why he is always so bubbly and humble. That's a fruit of complete trust in the Lord. When you trust that God is always in charge and knows what He is doing at all times, it brings peace to even the bleakest situations.

Maybe You're Ready to Tell Everyone You Know

The third thing you may be thinking is that you're excited about these truths and can't wait to share them with everyone you know. If this is you, let me caution you. Walk before you run. I recall being so excited to share what I just learned that I made phone calls to people in my Sunday school class, urging them to attend so I could enlighten them. I knew everyone would come to see what I've seen. It might take persistence, but eventually, everyone would see the light of the truth. Right?

> You never know where someone is on their journey, and exploring and discovering the truth is without doubt a journey.

Well, it's taken a few gray hairs and a few lost friends, but the answer is, *Wrong*. Not everyone will see what you see. Not everyone reading my words will explore for themselves, and certainly not everyone will see the truth as I see it. I've come to terms with that. It took me a few years to practice what I've preached. God is sovereign over all and He has everyone exactly where He wants them.

We all serve God's purpose whether we realize it or not. My

mission is to spread the freeing message of grace and sovereignty, but there are many missions and purposes that have nothing to do with understanding theology and doctrine. The nurse who prayed with your elderly relative may or may not have a complete grasp on the things I write about, but nonetheless served God. The neighbor who brought you dinner when you were sick may or may not know where to find certain verses in the Bible, but still serves the Lord. The mission worker may or may not know who wrote the book of Ephesians, but hands out Bibles anyway. I've accepted my mission. We're all called to serve differently, and my calling is to spread these truths.

You never know—one of you out there may also be called to join me in that effort. So, if you are, when you run into somebody who doesn't want to listen or believes you're full of baloney, don't try to wrestle them to the ground and make them agree. I tried that and it doesn't work. Smile and agree to disagree, and rest assured God has them right where He wants them. You never know where someone is on their journey, and exploring and discovering the truth is without a doubt a journey. It's when you can smile and see God at work in everything, and be thankful in any and all situations, especially the ones you don't understand—that's the ultimate sign of grace. He's got the whole world in His hands and, guess what, that includes you! *Amen.*

GOD IS NOT A MICROMANAGER • EVERYONE HAS THEIR OWN FREE WILL • THERE ARE
ROADS TO HEAVEN • WHEN WE DIE WE BECOME ANGELS • GOD HELPS THOSE WHO HELP
ELVES • GOD WANTS YOU TO BE RICH • CHRISTIANS AREN'T PERFECT, JUST FORGIVEN •
E GOD'S CO-PILOTS • PRAY HARD AND GOD WILL ANSWER • GOD AND SATAN ARE BATTLING
• GOD IS NOT A MICROMANAGER • EVERYONE HAS THEIR OWN FREE WILL • THERE ARE
ROADS TO HEAVEN • WHEN WE DIE WE BECOME ANGELS • GOD HELPS THOSE WHO HELP
ELVES • GOD WANTS YOU TO BE RICH • CHRISTIANS AREN'T PERFECT, JUST FORGIVEN •
E GOD'S CO-PILOTS • PRAY HARD AND GOD WILL ANSWER • GOD AND SATAN ARE BATTLING

More Beliefs to Explore and Examine

Before you exhale completely, I want to pull back the curtain a bit and let you know that the decision on which beliefs to include in this book wasn't an easy one. As I've mentioned, there are many more popular beliefs out there that are simply not true, even though people think they're in the Bible. There was an abundance of material to choose from. I chose the ones where I believe the truth has the greater impact on your Christian walk. With that said, I do acknowledge that it was a subjective process and that it might be helpful to you if I share a few of the beliefs that didn't make the cut.

The Big Payback

I mentioned in a previous chapter the notion that "What you are is God's gift to you, but what you make of yourself is your gift to God." This is misleading on several levels. First, you cannot, should not, will not, and could not ever begin to pay God back for what He's done for you. Under a payback system, your debt would be so great that there wouldn't be enough pages to hold all the zeros. The idea that a person should even attempt to pay God back is an insult to grace.

Second, it implies that God makes provisions for those who do good works, which is completely contrary to grace. I chose not to make this belief one of the ten, not because it isn't important to understand the truth, but simply because it so closely borders other beliefs I did write about, specifically "God helps those who help themselves." The belief that God's favor can be swayed by human effort is one that hopefully I've debunked enough earlier in this book.

There is, however, a story I'd like to tell that will clearly show the absurdity of trying to pay God back or earn your way to heaven.* It's one of those stories that have been told and retold countless times because they illustrate a point so well.

> A man was standing before Saint Peter at the Pearly Gates. Peter told the man that he needed 1000 points to get into heaven and asked the man what he had done to earn the points required. The man thought for a long time, trying to decipher which deeds were worth more points. He was a goodhearted man, though, and he was confident he could easily come up with 1000 points, so he began to list his good works.
>
> "Well, I was raised in the church. My father was a pastor and I never rebelled. I was president of my youth group. I went to a Bible college and then to a Christian graduate school. I was always active in my church. I didn't just talk religion either, I lived it. I gave over 30 percent of my income to the work of the kingdom. I never had a drink of alcohol, never lied that I can remember, was never arrested for any crime, and was a witness for Christ in every stage of my life.
>
> "I was married to the same woman for over 40 years. I never cheated on her and was always sensitive to her needs. We had three children, two girls and a boy. One girl is married to a preacher, the other is serving on a mission field overseas with her husband, and my son is now studying for the ministry at

---

* I ran across this story many years ago while reading a publication put out by Steve Brown of Key Life Ministries. I trust that Steve had found it many years before as well.

a well-known seminary. I always supported my pastor. I was an elder in the church for over 20 years and attended Sunday school, Sunday morning, Sunday evening, and Wednesday evening services regularly. I supported missionaries and often visited them on the field to encourage them. I was a bank president and tried to be a good citizen in my community, supporting the poor, working the prison ministry, and offering low-interest loans to those most in need."

Pausing, the man looked up at Peter and said, "How am I doing?" Peter answered, "Well, that's about one and a half points so far." The man cried out, "Good Lord, have mercy!" Peter laughed and said, "Now you've got it...come on in."

The Big 10 and the Big 3

That leads me to another popular belief that didn't quite make the cut: "People who keep the Ten Commandments will go to heaven." This, too, I've addressed along with other beliefs earlier in the book. Only perfect people go to heaven. We can read in James 2:10, "Whoever shall keep the whole law, and yet stumble in one point, he is guilty of all."

This also shoots down the prevalent notion that some sins are worse than others. It seems that for many Christians, as long as you stay away from the "Big 3" sins, you're okay (the Big 3 being murder, drinking, and adultery). I've known churches that have all but ostracized a member for an affair while turning a blind eye to what they perceive as lesser evils. The truth is very clear, however. All sins may not be equal in the eyes of humans, but they're all equal in the eyes of God. Break one tiny part of the law and you're guilty of breaking all of it. (To refresh your recollection of what I wrote about previously, according to Jesus, if you get angry with someone, you've committed murder. If you look at someone with lust in your heart, you've committed adultery.*)

---

* The Sermon on the Mount, Matthew 5.

You can't be perfect by trying to keep the law. The law was given for one reason, and that was to point us to Christ. (I wrote more extensively on this truth in *7 Biblical Truths You Won't Hear in Church*.) The law was our tutor to lead us to Jesus. Think of the law as a road sign that reads like this:

Give up?
Turn this way to Christ.

The only way we become perfect is through the blood of Christ. Through Him, we become blameless and have eternal life. The Ten Commandments are wonderful laws to govern our earthly experience, but they hold no value in getting us into heaven. Jesus is the only way to get that ticket punched!

Taking a Fall

Another notion I've heard bantered around the water cooler is that you can never be 100 percent certain of your salvation. I've heard people use the passage in Hebrews 6:6 as evidence of "falling from grace." But this is a classic case of using a single passage to support misguided theology. If you read the full text of Hebrews 6, the meaning is clear. Beginning in verse 4 the writer says,

> It is impossible for those who were once enlightened, and have tasted the heavenly gift, and have become partakers of the Holy Spirit, and have tasted the good word of God and the powers of the age to come [and now for verse 6], if they fall away to renew them again to repentance, since they crucify again for themselves the Son of God and put Him to an open shame.

This passage is not saying we can fall away, it is saying it is *impossible* to fall away. A couple more verses underscore the truth that once you become a new creation in Christ, you will not and cannot lose your salvation. In John 10:28-29 Jesus says,

I give them eternal life, and they shall never perish; neither shall anyone snatch them out of My hand. My Father who has given them [referring to all believers] to Me is greater than all; and no one is able to snatch them out of My Father's hand.

Finally, Romans 8:38 reads,

I am persuaded that neither death nor life, nor angels, nor principalities, nor powers, nor things present or things to come, nor height, nor depth, nor any other created thing ·shall be able to separate us from the love of God which is in Christ Jesus our Lord.

Those are pretty definitive statements—and ones that should give you total peace that your place with God in eternity is 100 percent safe and secure.

Surrender—What Is It?

I came real close to adding the popular belief that says you must surrender to Jesus. I've heard several versions of this, and it is a quite popular sermon topic. I must admit, this one drives me nuts. For starters, I could not find this anywhere in the New Testament. If it was something we as believers were called to do, don't you think it would be mentioned somewhere?

But even more perplexing than that is the question, What does surrendering to Jesus look like? I mean, how exactly do you do it? And more importantly, how do you know if you're completely surrendered? The obvious answer is, you can't. You might feel "surrendered" at one moment, and then "not surrendered" the next. This is a classic case of a popular belief that can and will frustrate believers. Don't get me wrong—as with a lot of the beliefs in this book, I get the concept. It's good to humble yourself before Jesus. I even wrote about the significance and importance of humility. If that's what is meant by surrendering, I'm okay with it, but most Christians define it as much more.

I asked a few of my close friends what it meant to surrender to Jesus and they couldn't come to a consensus. Most described it as setting aside their own will and accepting the will of Jesus. Based on my previous chapter on free will, my opposition to this contention is clear. Allow me to recap just a bit. As born-again, regenerated new creations in Christ, who have the mind and spirit of Christ indwelling us, there is simply no need for surrender. Our will was surrendered at the time of our conversion. End of debate. I only chose not to make this misguided belief its own chapter because it closely aligns with the idea of free will, but as you can tell, it gets my blood pumping!

The Impossible Standard

The most difficult decision, however, regarding inclusion came on the belief surrounding the very popular phrase "What Would Jesus Do?" or "WWJD" for short. The only reason I chose against it was because I also wrote about it in *7 Biblical Truths,* but let me recap a few of my concerns. Let me state for the record that philosophically WWJD is a noble belief. I can understand how it became so popular. My own daughter wore a WWJD bracelet for several years. And if it truly helps people make better decisions, I am all for it.

However, it is bad theology for three reasons. First, from history we can see it is impossible for people to be able to gauge what Jesus would do. When you thought Jesus would be in the temple, he was hanging out with tax collectors (who in those times were on the same level with criminals). When you thought he would rush to aid the sick, he lingered, as was the case with Lazarus. When you thought he would be in prayer and meditation, he was overturning tables and causing a scene. Jesus was completely unpredictable.

The second concern I have over WWJD is that it is in the "flesh cleanup" business. The idea that a person must continually be weighing their decisions and actions against the unachievable standard set by Jesus is not only frustrating and demoralizing—it can rob a believer of joy and peace. Let me say this as loudly and clearly as possible: Flesh is not capable of being cleaned up. You can dress it up in fancy clothes, but it will always be a tramp. You can cover it up with expensive perfume, but it will always rot and will die in the end. That's why flesh gets sick, old, and wrinkly, and why, once our spirit departs, flesh decays and turns to dust. God made man out of dust and when flesh dies, it returns to dust. This is what David meant when he wrote in Psalm 104:29, "You take away their breath; they die and return to their dust."

Flesh is not what is redeemed. Flesh is not what is born again. Flesh is not capable of doing good. This is what Isaiah meant when he wrote in Isaiah 64:6, We are all like an unclean thing, and all our righteousnesses are like filthy rags." The only way to become righteous is, not by trying to clean up the flesh, but by turning to Jesus. WWJD often misdirects us toward doing good instead of turning to Him. I interviewed a teenage girl one time as to why she was wearing the WWJD bracelet. She told me it was so others, particularly boys, would know she's a Christian. That all sounds good enough, but when I asked her if she was a Christian, she answered by saying, "I think I do more good things than bad things." A bracelet and a catchy slogan aren't enough. Cleaning up flesh is a hollow proposition. It's like putting lipstick on a corpse. Jesus is the only answer to becoming righteous. He is truly all you need.

> Too many sins become obsessions because we keep them hidden and try to overcome them through self-effort.

My friend Glenna Salsbury has a unique and refreshing alternative to WWJD and trying to clean up flesh. Instead of teaching people to conquer their sins and weaknesses, she teaches people to embrace them! (Sounds shocking, right? I'll explain in a moment.) I've heard her counsel others to not hide their sins and pretend they don't exist, but rather to embrace them and even give thanks to God for revealing them so plainly.

Her advice is sound. When something is taboo and kept hidden, it is destined to increase and be repeated. Tell a child you've hid cookies until after dinner, and that will only make the child want the cookie more. Take away the taboo and the cookie won't seem quite as desirable. Sure, the child may still eat the cookie, but the cookie will remain just a cookie. It won't become an obsession. Too many sins become obsessions because we keep them hidden and try to overcome them through self-effort. Again, sin cannot be overcome through the work of the flesh.

Embracing them doesn't mean that you should love them or like them. Embracing them simply means to acknowledge them and turn them over to Jesus. He alone is the only change agent. Embrace your sins and, amazingly, you will be freed from their grip.

Lastly, WWJD denies a believer their true identity. My dear friend and fellow writer Steve McVey once said that instead of WWJD standing for What Would Jesus Do, it should stand for *Watch What Jesus Does!* We don't need to wonder what Jesus would do because, as believers, we have the mind of Christ. We don't need to live wondering if we've made the right decisions to live *for* Jesus—He will live *through* us. As Steve said in his tape series, "How to Know and Do the Will of God,"

> Not only will Jesus Christ live through us, He will *think* through us as well. The determining issue in doing God's will isn't "placing a fleece before the Lord," but instead trusting in the truth that our sovereign God will fulfill His purpose through us. Our response is to trust in Him, believing that He will guide our thoughts and actions so that every detail of His plan will be executed. Don't worry over God's will. Just trust Him, make your decision, and then act in faith. It is His responsibility and pleasure to see to it that you do His perfect will. So, relax and enjoy the journey.

Well said!

I could name a few more popular beliefs, but they all seem to be restating the same things. (It seems like it's always that way with human ideas.) The bottom line to most popular beliefs is that they give too much power and credit to man and not enough to God. Instead of so much focus on empowering man, why isn't there more teaching and celebration that ascribes power to God?

For too many people, God is too small. This book, if nothing else, is an attempt to help you see and understand a sovereign God who is bigger, more wonderful, more in control, and more worthy of awe than we can possibly imagine. When the day comes that we find ourselves standing before the throne of the Lord, I'd rather err on the side of giving God too much credit than not enough. I'd rather say, "Gosh, Lord, I should have taken more credit," than, "Gosh, God, I took too much credit."

You know what? I don't believe you can give God too much credit. He's older, wiser, stronger, more in control, more experienced, and more powerful. He has an impeccable resume. He's the Alpha and Omega, the author and finisher of our faith, Creator of all things, King of kings, Lord of lords, Master...Father, Son, and Holy Spirit. Our God is truly an awesome God.

NOTES

Chapter 2—Belief # 1: There Are Many Roads to Heaven
1. Isaiah 55:8.
2. See Luke 23:39-43.

Chapter 3—Belief #2: When We Die, We Become Angels
1. Hebrews 13:2.

Chapter 4—Belief #3: God Helps Those Who Help Themselves
1. I know it may be a dying profession, but I know a shoe cobbler in my hometown and he's an awesome individual. He's saved me on more than a few occasions, from repairing a shoe to fixing my son's leather baseball glove.

Chapter 6—Belief #5: Christians Aren't Perfect, Just Forgiven
1. Colossians 3:3 and Romans 6:6 are good verses to support this truth.
2. Steve's books include *Grace Walk*, *The Grace Walk Experience*, *Grace Rules*, and *Grace Amazing*.

Chapter 7—Belief #6: We Are God's Co-Pilots
1. Isaiah 45:7 KJV.
2. We don't clearly know what kind of fruit the Tree of the Knowledge of Good and Evil bore. Pop culture has come to believe the forbidden fruit was an apple, but Scripture doesn't tell us outright. All we know is that the fruit was appealing to the eye.
3. 2 Corinthians 12:10.

Chapter 8—Belief #7: Pray Hard and God Will Answer
1. Romans 11:36. Note again the words "all things."

Chapter 9—Belief #8: God and Satan Are Battling It Out
1. Job 1:8.

Chapter 11—Belief #10: Everyone Has Their Own Free Will
1. Isaiah 59:2.
2. 1 Corinthians 2:16.
3. 1 Corinthians 2:16 and 1 Corinthians 6:17.
4. Also see Romans 5:5.

Chapter 12—Another Reformation
1. Just for the record, it's found in Matthew 5.
2. *World Christian Encyclopedia*, 2nd ed., January 2001, Oxford Press.

Invite David Rich to Speak at
Your Church or at Your Next Event!

Popular presentations from David

Contagious Peace!

This presentation can be anywhere from a 20-minute sermon to a one-hour keynote. "Contagious Peace" focuses on one of the truths of David's book, *7 Biblical Truths You Won't Hear in Church...But Might Change Your Life*. You choose the topic according to your needs and congregation or audience. The end result of each truth is to bring the believer closer to God so they can enter the rest as Jesus commanded and to enjoy the most sought-after commodity on earth: peace. Peace in knowing the truth will set you free and is highly contagious!

The "7 Truths" Seminar

This is David's full workshop on the seven truths in his book. The workshop is five hours and can be held as a one-day Saturday event (typically 10 to 4 with a one-hour lunch break) or split between two sessions over a Friday evening and Saturday morning. This is an interactive, Bibles-open exploration of the seven truths. This is for the church or Christian organization that isn't afraid to challenge their members as to what they believe and why. The goal is not to convince people that what they may have believed their entire lives is wrong, but rather to drive them to the Word for deeper doctrinal understanding and conviction for the truth.

Visit www.GraceCamp.com for more information.

Also by David Rich

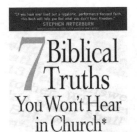

Did Somebody Leave Out
the Good Parts?

You may have listened to hundreds of sermons and gotten
some good practical advice at church, but perhaps the
Christianity you've encountered just doesn't seem *life-changing*.

What you're not hearing, though, can be crucial, says
author David Rich. Fast-paced and straightforward,
David challenges you with seven scriptural truths that
are key to significance and fulfillment in your spiritual
life, such as...

- trying to live for Jesus will only frustrate you

- what you see in the mirror is not what God sees

- the Ten Commandments were not meant to be kept

The truth is still there for you to hear. You may be surprised by it—but as you take
it in, you may also find peace, contentment, and friendship with God that you
never expected to get from being a Christian.

To read a sample chapter, go to
www.harvesthousepublishers.com

New Horizons in Spiritual Growth

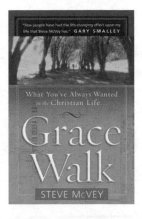

GRACE WALK

Steve McVey

Nothing you have ever done, nothing you could ever do, will match the incomparable joy of letting Jesus live His life through you. It is what makes the fire of passion burn so brightly in new believers. And it is what causes the light of contentment to shine in the eyes of mature believers who have learned the secret of the *Grace Walk*.

If you know how to live it, you'll be strengthened by the depth of Steve McVey's insights. If you long for it, you can begin today!

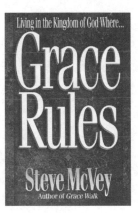

GRACE RULES

Steve McVey

Are you "living by the rules"...or are you letting God's grace rule you?

There's a big difference. If you're living *for* God—living by the rules—you'll always be exhausted. You'll feel as if you're not doing enough for Him... and that if you don't "measure up," He'll be displeased with you.

But God never meant for you to live the Christian life that way! His love for you isn't based on how you perform for Him. He sent Christ to set you free from rules. He didn't call you to serve Him in your own feeble power...but to let *His* limitless power flow through you!

Find out how to rest in His grace and let Him live through you in *Grace Rules*.

If Your Christian Life Seems as Dry as Dust
and You're Just Going Around in Circles...
Maybe You're Wandering in the Wilderness

In the wilderness, you feel as though...

- you live by the rules, and the Bible is the rule book
- you work hard for God...but you never quite measure up
- you have to get your act together first—then God grants you His blessings

In the land of God's amazing grace, you experience the truth that...

- God has made you alive *in Christ*—and now you want to do what He wants
- Jesus has done all the work, and you can rest in the Father's acceptance
- God has already given you every spiritual blessing, and now you can live in freedom and confidence

Using the story of Israel's journey out of the desert and arrival in the Promised Land as a backdrop, Steve McVey reveals to you more of the heart of your loving, giving Father...so you can better grasp just why His grace is so amazing.

"I strongly urge you to get Becoming Who God Intended
and put it to work in your life."

Becoming Who God Intended

*A New Picture for Your Past • A Healthy
Way of Managing Your Emotions • A Fresh
Perspective on Relationships*

DAVID ECKMAN

Whether you realize it or not, your imagination is filled with *pictures* of reality. The Bible indicates these pictures reveal your true "heart beliefs"—the beliefs that actually shape your everyday feelings and reactions to family, friends, and others, to life's circumstances, and to God.

David Eckman compassionately shows you how to allow God's Spirit to build new, *biblical* pictures in your heart and imagination. As you do this, you will be able to accept God's acceptance of you in Christ, break free of negative emotions and habitual sin…and finally experience the life God the Father has always intended for you.

*"David Eckman is a man you can trust…
His teaching resonates with God's wisdom and compassion."*

—STU WEBER, author of *Tender Warrior*
and *Four Pillars of a Man's Heart*

*To read a sample chapter, go to
www.harvesthousepublishers.com*